THE CRAFT OF FOOD AND COOKERY WRITING

THE CRAFT OF FOOD AND COOKERY WRITING

Janet Laurence

ALLISON & BUSBY

First published in 1994 by
Allison & Busby
an imprint of Wilson & Day Ltd
5 The Lodge
Richmond Way
London W12 8LW

Copyright © Janet Laurence 1994

The moral right of the author has been asserted

ISBN 074900 211 5

Typeset by TW Typesetting, Plymouth, Devon
Printed and bound by Biddles, Guildford

CONTENTS

To
Janet Clarke
for opening my eyes to so many aspects
of food and cookery books, not only
historical ones

ACKNOWLEDGEMENTS

I owe many people a debt of gratitude for taking the time from their busy schedules to discuss many aspects of food and cookery writing. In particular I would like to thank Pepita Aris, Lynda Brown, Anna Del Conte, Clarissa Dickson-Wright, Anne Dolamore, Sara-Jane Evans, Clare Ferguson, Rosemary Moon, Anna Powell, Margaret Shaida, Drew Smith, Michael Thomas and Robin Weir. For information on printing and self-publishing, I am indebted to Charles Dewey of Postscript Publishing, Bath; Alan Bishop and Alison Roelich of Haynes Publishing, Sparkford; and Tessa Warburg.

1

QUALIFICATIONS AND POSSIBILITIES

So you want to write about food – bravo!

Food is basic to our existence, a necessity; we all have to eat to live. Food can also be a joyful experience and an art form. On another level, food is surrounded with social, psychological and religious significance. It is difficult to think of a subject easier to get interested in, or one on which you are more likely to be qualified to write.

Check through any cook's bookshelf and there will be tattered and greasy books, sometimes almost falling to pieces. Those are the ones the cook returns to time and again because the recipes work, they fulfil a need, and are inspirational.

No one can tell you how to develop such recipes but cookery writing has certain conventions which can be learned by anyone interested and this book aims to identify them. I hope also to give an idea of the scope there is for writers interested in food and cookery; it is far from being a narrow specialisation. The book also assesses the requirements necessary and the chances for success in various areas.

The scope for writers interested in food and cookery

We are very lucky in Great Britain today because the interest there has been in food over the last few years means that most people are open to new ideas. Pasta, Chinese stir-fry,

Indian spices, Mexican hot peppers and many other exotica are now commonplace in our daily diet. Not only that, but there is a wide audience eager for more information on ingredients, production of food, health and nutrition, and ways of producing an enormous variety of dishes and meals.

So, even though food and cookery can be seen as a specialist area, it is one that offers a wide range of approaches and can offer the beginner excellent opportunities for breaking into print. Yes, there is a lot of competition, but there are also editors and publishers eager for new writers who can offer fresh ideas and original recipes.

Recipe based writing is perhaps the food angle that springs to most people's minds. We've all scanned articles and bought books hoping to be inspired into producing new dishes for family or friends, and the demand for these new ideas is endless.

If you have ambitions in this direction, this book covers the development of ideas into articles and books, the technical aspects of recipe writing, recipe copyright, illustrations and other features.

It is not only the dedicated cook, though, who can profit from an interest in this area. Food offers many approaches that aren't recipe based at all and which can be very attractive to the general writer.

Some possible angles or approaches have already been mentioned and there are others.

The historical aspect, for instance. The question of what our ancestors ate, how it was produced, cooked and served and what it reveals about social and other habits of the time, offers interesting possibilities for a writer. Perhaps you have an interesting manuscript recipe book from a previous century and are wondering if it couldn't be published in some way.

There are medical, social and psychological theories regarding food, its preparation and consumption, which can be fascinating.

The cultural, geographical and climatic parameters of food offer, if you will excuse the pun, another fertile field for writers.

2

Once you start exploring, in fact, the possible angles are endless.

For writers, food and cookery also offer a possible bonus which is not enjoyed by any other area of writing, usually a lonely experience. Whether it is the fruits of research or recipe testing, writing about food nearly always involves consuming something – and what is more fun than to share it with friends? Sometimes, indeed, it is essential to have the opinion of others on a particular food or dish. If you are able to pass on the expenses, you can entertain for nothing. Even if you can't, you may be able to put the cost against income for tax purposes.

Food and cookery is also a field that attracts people not necessarily ambitious to break into commercial publishing.

Who hasn't been offered, and bought, a spiral-bound paperback of recipes being sold on behalf of some charity? Perhaps you're now looking at the possibility of producing one yourself.

Or maybe you hope to collect together recipes, not as a commercial proposition, but for family and friends. With modern printing techniques, this need not be a very expensive proposition and can offer great scope to eager eaters anxious to pass on the fruits of their tables.

Self-publication can also offer opportunities to the commercial writer. It is not something to be embarked upon lightly but the possibilities are covered in Chapter Eleven.

Qualifications

Do you need to be a *cordon bleu* cook to write a recipe book? There are many, many cookery writers who have produced classic books without ever having had a formal lesson in their lives. Some of the great modern writers, such as Elizabeth David and Jane Grigson, for instance, are among them.

Maybe you have disasters and think that these disqualify you. Far from it. If you produce a soufflé that doesn't rise, then find out *why* and work out rules that bring foolproof results, you are probably better equipped to write a recipe and explain the technique to a beginner than someone who has never had a failure.

Don't be daunted by not having a cookery diploma or a home economics degree. There are editors who believe that a formal training hampers creativity.

Still worried you are not qualified? Take a look at this list and consider whether:

- You produce food people like to eat
- You love cooking
- You have a deep interest in a particular aspect of food
- You love to eat
- You have an enquiring mind

If you can answer yes to one or more of the above, you could be qualified to write about food or cookery. If you can answer 'yes' to all of them, you should be able to launch into book or article with every chance of success.

What the successful writer *does* need are the following:

- An endless capacity for hard work
- The ability to take rejection and come back for more
- The persistence and patience to ensure that every fact, every detail and every recipe is checked and rechecked
- The determination never to be satisfied with the pedestrian or second-rate
- The imagination to see new possibilities and approaches to everyday subjects
- The intelligence to research markets and angle work to suit them

Henrietta Green summed it all up by identifying her background as a cookery writer as, 'Years of hard work and research and a deeply serious greed'.

Still interested? Good. Let's take a look at the prospects for the dedicated food and cookery writer.

4

Opportunities

Over the last ten years or so, public interest in food has exploded. Magazines have been launched dealing with nothing but food, more and more books have been published on the subject and there is hardly a magazine or newspaper that does not have a food or cookery column of some sort.

A glittering prospect for the would-be writer.

I have to say, however, that these golden opportunities are fought for by large numbers of talented and hard-working writers. It is a very, very competitive field.

That doesn't mean there aren't openings for new writers.

One very experienced cookery journalist I talked to recently was despondent over the difficulty of getting articles accepted. So few openings, she said. Yet, the next day, I spoke to another journalist, equally experienced, who felt that the number of outlets was so enormous that persistence was bound to pay off. Is a jug half full or half empty?

Because food is a subject of such universal interest and is attractive to so many people, it naturally appeals to many writers. But an experienced journalist very often wants to make sure that there is a commission before putting pen to paper. The eager beginner is often more willing to take a chance and submit an unsolicited article which may be accepted.

The writer who is persistent (and I can't put enough emphasis on this word), who continually studies his market and who works at producing original and lively articles, has every chance of finding an increasing number of outlets for his work.

Incidentally, throughout this book, though many food and cookery writers and editors are female, I use the generic 'he' rather than say 'he or she' every time.

The book market is perhaps a little more difficult than the article market, yet, despite the number of food and cookery books published, or perhaps because of it, publishers are always on the lookout for new ideas. As Chapter Four explains, beginners have as much of a chance as experienced writers, if their ideas and approach are right.

If recipe based writing is what attracts you, one of the new entrées is to win a national cookery competition. Television's *MasterChef*, and the competitions run by various newspapers, offer unknowns a nerve-wracking but instant road to success. Nicola Cox, Frances Bissell, Jeremy Round, Brian Glover, Lynda Brown and Sue Lawrence are just a few of the writers who got their start through winning one of these competitions. If you feel you could cope with the pressures, it could prove a lucrative way in. If you don't win the first time round, try again. Anyone involved in organising these competitions will tell you that the same names crop up again and again – and that persistence often pays off.

Similarly, there are competitions for food writing. Two are organised by the Guild of Food Writers whose address is given in the Appendix.

One of the most effective ways into food and cookery writing is to become known for a specialisation. Food from a particular country (the more unknown the better), vegetarian cooking, up market presentation ideas, organic farming, special diets and nutrition are just a few possible areas that editors and readers could be interested in. Maybe you don't have a specialist interest at the moment – but you may be able to find one, perhaps with the help of this book.

Breaking into recipe writing can sometimes be made easier by teaming up with a food photographer. Producing both the words and illustrations can simplify an editor's job and means your work stands a better chance of acceptance. This point is covered in more detail in Chapter Nine.

If you can claim cookery qualifications, you may be able to learn how a magazine works by offering your services, free, to a specialist food publication with a kitchen. Their reward is an extra pair of skilled hands. It's an excellent way to get a flavour of how a magazine is created and what it looks for from its contributors, and you need only do a couple of days. You might find them interested in ideas of yours as well.

If you are in any way involved with food already, perhaps as a home economist or stylist, maximise any contact with editors of publications or publishing houses. Working on other people's recipes for photography sessions has allowed more than one stylist to develop into a cookery writer. Equally, helping other writers prepare recipes for publication can mean opportunities for contact with publishers. Always be on the lookout for legitimate ways of presenting your own ideas and don't pass up any of them.

Cooking for magazines can be another way in. Annie Bell, one of our newer cookery writers, was a caterer and got her chance to submit articles after she had supplied *Vogue* with her delicious food.

Networking can also help. Food people are, on the whole, extremely friendly. Because so much of our work is concerned with the consumption of food, meetings are often convivial and highly enjoyable. There are a number of symposia concerned with food where new voices are welcomed and valuable contacts can be made. Watch in the media for announcements regarding The Oxford Symposium on Food & Cookery, the daddy of them all, and others. Competition for places is keen but usually there are no particular qualifications required. Symposiasts are invited to give a paper on some aspect of the current theme. The prospect may be daunting but this is a splendid opportunity to make a mark with a scintillating, erudite or novel approach. An editor may well remember your name later when you submit an article or an idea. Your work still has to make the grade but you will have a head start for his attention.

The opportunities are out there. You just have to make the most of them!

What are your aims?

When starting out, many people are rather vague about exactly what they want to achieve. Do you know what your aims are?

Some readers will know exactly what their ambition is.

Perhaps there is a book they want to write, a collection of recipes to edit for a charity cookbook or they have formulated clear ideas for articles.

If you fall into this group, congratulations! You know exactly where you are going and you can skip the rest of this section.

Perhaps, though, your aims aren't so easily identified.

You love cooking and reading about food and are wondering whether you have the ability to take your interests further.

You've always thought about making a collection of your favourite recipes, you're sure many other people would love them as you do and you're wondering whether they could make a book.

You want to become a writer, and food appeals to you as a subject for your pen – but you have no particular field of interest.

Now is the time to look more closely at your ambitions.

With any venture, it always helps to define exactly what you hope to achieve. Goals give you something to aim for. More than that, if you know where you want to go, you can sort out what you need to get there and what the various stages are.

So now is the time to look more closely at your ambitions and identify at least one goal. Then you can tackle the rest of this book with a positive aim in mind.

Don't shrink from setting your sights high. The higher you aim, the more likely you are to get at least somewhere near your target. Settle for something modest and you are unlikely to get very far.

Here are some possible targets:

- A cookery book published
- A book on a particular aspect of food published
- A reputation established as a reliable writer of food or cookery articles
- A successful fund-raising cookery book produced
- A book for family and friends written and produced

You might have more than one of these targets in mind. You might want to write both articles and books, for instance. You don't have to define exactly what sort of book or article you want to write at this stage, Chapters Three, Four and Five look at this subject in detail. But you do need to identify in which direction you want to be moving.

How to achieve your target

Any ambition starts out as a dream and becomes reality through a series of simple stages:

- Identification of target
- Preparation
- Perseverance

You've decided what you want to do. Now you must do your research, both into the market for your work, whether it is for articles or a book, and the background information needed for that work. You then need to assemble it all into suitable shape. Organisation is what this book is all about.

What no book can do, however, is give you the perseverance to keep on trying – no matter how hard the going gets or how often you are rejected. Nor can it provide that extra effort which means your work has the edge on the competition. You must provide this yourself and that is the toughest part.

2

GETTING YOURSELF ORGANISED

Information is the life-blood of any writer, and organisation is essential to ensure that you are able to make the most of your resources and your research. A little discipline will mean your writing can benefit from a wide range of information. Some of this you will already have on hand, and a great deal will be gathered from various forms of research. All your information will need organising so that you know what you have – and can find what you want when you want it.

Your background information can be broken down into various categories:

- Notes
- Contact names and addresses
- Cuttings
- Books

Notes

Notes can be taken at any time, in any place. Always carry a small notebook and pen or pencil, as you never know when you may want to record something interesting and food offers more opportunities than probably any other subject for unexpected discoveries. Walk through a shopping area and you could discover a new food outlet, an unfamiliar ingredient or a restaurant offering an unusual menu. A drive in the country may lead you to a notice-board advertising a promising farm or food supplier. Go into any pub or restaurant for the most ordinary of meals and you may discover an unexpected dish or approach to food. Travel abroad and the opportunities are even greater because more is likely to be out of the ordinary.

Always be on the look out for possibly interesting information. Wandering through Birmingham Art Gallery recently, I found an extremely well labelled and annotated display of traditional gingerbread moulds. Out came my notebook and I copied down the information together with detailed notes on the moulds, the name of the art gallery and the date of my visit. At the moment I have no idea what I shall do with these notes but my mind is working on various possibilities. It may be possible to tie them in with other historical references for an article for some sort of collectors' magazine. Or perhaps I will work on a gingerbread recipe article and use the notes as part of a colourful introduction. One thing I know for certain, if I'd just passed the display by or hadn't bothered to take down the details, I'd regret it at some stage.

Always take notes on eating experiences, both at home and abroad, with either home cooks or in restaurants. Even if a particular dish can be retained sharply in your memory, other details may fade. Taking notes, even if only mentally (there are many occasions when it is totally inappropriate to bring out a notebook), sharpens your taste buds. A restaurant critic I know works furiously hard at assessing dishes as he and friends taste them. Afterwards, he sits in his car outside the restaurant, writing everything down before he even puts his key in the ignition. As well as descriptions of the food, the service and the ambience of the restaurant, note also its name, address and telephone number, and any details you have gleaned about the chef, etc. These may all be needed.

While small notebooks are essential for this sort of notetaking, large notebooks can be preferable for other occasions. I use a quarto-sized hardbacked notebook for research visits for two reasons: first, large books are harder to put down and forget than small ones; second, their pages have more room to make the sort of diagrammatic notes that can sort out information as you go along (*see* Figure 1). This way of taking notes, marked with dates and contact names, addresses and telephone numbers, can also identify other possible angles for which you could use the information. Always maximise your research. When your notebook is full, label it with the dates of the period it covers and keep it safe for future reference.

Always make sure that your own name, address and telephone number are on the cover of each notebook, just in case you leave it anywhere.

Try and write up notes as soon as possible, when it is still easy to flesh them out. Also, if your writing is difficult to read (and sometimes these notes are made under difficult conditions), it's easier to decipher it when you can remember what the subject matter was!

I write my notes up on a word processor and then file a hard copy in a ring binder. Some people have systems of reference numbers to identify back to the right file or disk – but I don't bother, because complicated indexing systems can be time-consuming in themselves. But there *are* times when I regret not having an index. You must choose.

For interviews, a tape recorder can be very helpful, as long as the person you are talking to is not put off by its presence.

Machinery can offer problems. You need to make sure you have sufficient tapes and batteries for however long you feel the interview may last. You also need to check the machine before starting out and then be sure to press the 'Record' button. It sounds obvious but I forgot to do just that the other day. It meant a hectic session afterwards writing down everything I could remember from a fascinating conversation with an olive oil merchant.

If you are going to want to transcribe complete tapes on a regular basis, a foot-operated gadget that will stop and start the cassette, such as audio typists use, is a worthwhile investment.

Keep tapes. They don't cost very much – and you never know when you could find a replay valuable for a quotation or piece of information for another article. Always make sure

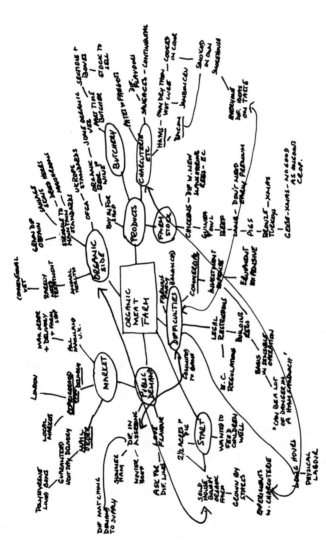

Notes taken at an organic farm. Initially these were used as a basis for a crime novel I wrote centred on an organic farm. Later I returned to them and identified the possibility of an article on the farmer in the 'Slice of Life' series run by *Taste Magazine*. The idea was accepted, I revisited the farmer and the article duly appeared.

your tapes are clearly identified with dates, interviewee name/s, addresses and telephone numbers.

Photographs or sketches can provide visual notes and, possibly, illustrations for an article or book (*see* Chapter Nine). Always carry a camera, for it can capture in an instant what would otherwise take many words to describe. Identify prints and negatives clearly with subject, place and date.

Photographs can also provide reference details of ingredients and dishes. They will probably not be good enough for publication but can record how an ingredient looked before you cooked it or capture the presentation of a dish. Chefs often use polaroid photos to ensure that each time a dish is prepared, it looks exactly right.

Much research can be done on the telephone, particularly when long distances are involved. Before calling, I write down the questions I want answered or the areas for discussion – it's very easy to get lost down interesting byways – and take copious notes during the conversation. Again, these are transcribed on to the processor immediately after the conversation is finished.

Reading can also yield information which may come in handy later. Noting down title, author and page number with a brief reminder of the gist of the information can save a great deal of searching later on. Such information can be filed on a word processor disk or in a notebook, looseleaf book or on cards.

Watching television or listening to the radio can also provide valuable information or ideas. Make sure a notebook and pencil are always available to hand so that you can record details as soon as you hear them. Again, identify the source and log the details as soon as possible.

As such information grows, it needs to be organised. Some people like card indexes. These can refer to files, books or other sources and be sorted alphabetically or into subject groups. Or you can use a computer or word processor. I like ring binders that can file a mixture of typed-up and hand-written notes.

Assembling information for a particular project, especially

for a large one such as a book, can require a mixture of systems. A card index can provide basic detail supported by notes, cuttings, photostats, etc., filed in anything from a proper cabinet to a cardboard box. What matters is that you should be able to find what you need, quickly.

Contact names and addresses

If you are writing about different aspects of food, you will need to build a file of contacts: food shops and other retail outlets, farmers, market gardeners, specialist producers, processors, suppliers of various commodities, chefs, good cooks of all kinds, and perhaps nutritionists, dieticians, etc.

It's easy to jot down names and addresses or file visiting cards in a filofax or notebook; however, nothing is more infuriating than coming across a name later and being unable to remember why it was important. A quick note made beside the name at the time you add it to your collection can be helpful. For instance: Jane Smith, organic poultry farmer, specialises in bronze turkeys for Xmas. A card index can then cross-reference the farmer under 'Smith', 'Organic farmer', 'poultry' and 'turkeys'.

If you have a full account of Jane Smith, add a note of where this is filed as well.

Sources for difficult-to-find ingredients, ethnic foods, for instance, or expensive items such as caviar or smoked eel, not often stocked by local suppliers, should also be noted. This is particularly important if you live in the country, when mail order firms can be useful. Time is always at a premium and having to search around, either by phone or car, to find something you need for testing a particular recipe can be immensely frustrating.

Along with names and addresses, note details such as quality of food, willingness to help, special attributes, etc.

If you like to carry all such information about with you in a personal organiser, do keep a copy at home. Handbags and briefcases are very vulnerable to theft and losing such valuable details can be shattering. If you are daunted by your filofax's bulging address section, head for your nearest photocopying outlet.

For the same reason, never neglect back-up files for information stored on a computer. Apart from occasions when discs with their load of valuable records become corrupted, computer theft becomes more commonplace every day. No insurance company can give you back your precious notes, recipes and other creative effort. Apart from back-up files, hard or printed out copies are also valuable for quick reference and for times when the computer is down.

Cuttings

Always check your newspapers and magazines for useful cuttings. Information on food and health, new developments, background stories on ingredients, chefs and other foodies, interesting recipes, details of producers and new products, may all be of no immediate use but could prove helpful at some stage in the future.

Cuttings should always be marked with the name of the newspaper and magazine where they come from, and the date. Unidentifiable references are of little use to the conscientious researcher.

File cuttings under suitable headings. You don't have to use a filing cabinet and hanging files, a cardboard box and used large envelopes will do perfectly well. Set the envelope on edge with a clearly marked heading at the top, or sellotape a strip of card so that it stands proud of the envelope. Once a file or envelope starts getting too fat, break the contents down into associated subjects or dates.

Try and go through cuttings files every so often and discard those no longer of use. This will not only keep the size of your collection under control, it will remind you of what information you have and may suggest ideas for articles.

Food magazines often have annual indexes, especially for recipes. Remove these and keep them to hand. Binders are sometimes available; otherwise, keep the magazines in date order and don't be afraid to take out interesting cuttings to file with your others. If you would rather not mutilate the magazine, write the reference on a piece of paper and file that with your cuttings, or enter it on a card index system.

A word of warning: check facts before using them, particularly if the cutting you are using is not a current one. Science moves on, up-to-date research produces new information that alters conclusions, careers change direction and what is the latest theory today is old hat tomorrow. Also, no one is infallible, least of all journalists under pressure, and just because you read something in a newspaper does not mean it is true. On the other hand, being under pressure is no excuse for your not getting your story right. A reputation for reliability is one of the most valuable things a writer can have. If your work proves suspect, editors are unlikely to trust you a second time.

Books

A reference library of your own can be an enormous help. For a food and cookery writer, quite apart from the usual dictionary, thesaurus, and grammar, etc., there are many different volumes that are useful to have on one's shelf.

Scientific and technical books can be alarming but a writer on food and cookery must understand basic cooking techniques and processes if his recipes are to avoid ambiguities and pitfalls for the inexperienced cook. A practical handbook that is a pleasure to read and a fund of fascinating information is Harold McGee's *On Food and Cooking – The Science and Lore of the Kitchen* (HarperCollins). If you want to know exactly what happens when bread dough is kneaded, what the role of nitrite is in preserving meats, or how to prevent greens losing their colour when cooked, for example, then Harold McGee is your man.

Diet is a complex subject, and needs extended study before individuals can consider themselves equipped to write about it in any depth. You should, though, be aware of what the basic nutritional requirements of the human body are according to the latest research and also understand current dietary issues; what exactly is 'the Mediterranean diet', for instance, or the difference between saturated, poly-unsaturated and mono-unsaturated fats? A basic nutrition handbook can be very useful and help to put media reports of new issues in context. Your library, or a scientific bookshop, should be able to recommend one that is up-to-date.

There are a number of very useful encyclopaedias of cooking ingredients. Understanding ingredients, where they originate from, how they are produced and what their properties are, etc., can help make your articles and books lively and interesting and also inspire new recipes. Tom Stobart's *The Cook's Encyclopaedia* (B. T. Batsford) is a book I refer to constantly and haven't found replaced by anything more comprehensive. It is supported on my shelves by a number of more specialised books.

All cooks will have a favourite general cookery book which reminds them of, for instance, the basic recipe for a Victoria sponge or puff pastry. Such recipes are eternal and provide the basis for any number of variations.

Equally helpful are books on classic haute cuisine. These are essential for an understanding of the dishes that provide the backbone of western cooking. Interested cooks probably have at least one such book on their shelves already.

Also of interest are books explaining different ethnic cuisines. Many of the ingredients necessary to cook these dishes can now be found in this country. Cooks such as Madhur Jaffrey, Sri Owen, Claudia Roden, Yan Kit So, and many others have inspired the use of traditional flavourings, ingredients and techniques from many parts of the world. Our cooking is richer for their help and no creative cook today can afford to ignore their contribution. To keep up with important newcomers, check with major bookshops and watch reviews of cookery books, television programmes and cookery columns which include recipes from new books.

Cookery books written by chefs can help with advanced techniques and presentations and give an insight into adventurous flavouring and new approaches to haute cuisine. Some present over-elaborate food that is a passing fad but the best can be inspirational.

Food is far more than the fuel that keeps us going. The past, approached through both recipe books and histories of food and its consumption, can give us insights into the development of eating and help us understand the complex interrelation that can exist between food and industrial, social, economic and other developments. An appreciation of these dimensions can add extra depth to your writing.

Books by what might be called the academic and philosophical food and cookery writers should also find a place on your shelves. *The Philosopher in the Kitchen* (Penguin) by Brillat Savarin, the French eighteenth-century philosopher, began a tradition of educated appraisal of food and its mores that has been continued in the second half of this century by a number of writers including M. F. K. Fisher, an American with a passionate interest in food. Her books are light on recipes but offer a highly intelligent and immensely readable look at many aspects of the food scene in both Europe and America. An academic voice from Canada currently making her mark is Margaret Visser. Then there are writers such as Elizabeth David and Jane Grigson who have inspired whole generations of cooks and also broadened our understanding of food.

Anthologies, collections of quotations and either short or long excerpts from other works can also be helpful, both for an indication of the wide range of food references available and for providing useful quotations for your own work.

Then, of course, there are books by cookery writers you yourself find particularly interesting and instructive. Cooking other people's recipes can extend your knowledge of how ingredients blend together, the versatility of certain techniques and suggest particularly successful uses of spices and other flavourings. Sometimes, reading other people's books can also demonstrate pitfalls to be avoided in choice of ingredients, method or the way a recipe is explained.

A good system for noting interesting details in a book, or recipes that you want to try at some stage, is to mark the right page with a slip of paper. It's easy to see and you can scribble one or two words on the slip to remind you of the reference.

Books are expensive and many interesting ones are out of print anyway. Make a habit of checking the food and cookery sections of any second-hand bookshops for bargains. Make friends with local ones and they will let you know when books come in that could interest you. There are antiquarian booksellers who specialise in food and these are particularly useful when tracking down special books. A list of the leading gastronomic antiquarian booksellers is included at the end of this book. They all issue catalogues at regular intervals and are willing to include new names on their mailing lists.

Another source of cheap books is the cut-price bookshop. Don't assume that these are all rubbish. So many cookery books are published these days that a certain percentage of excellent ones that haven't sold as quickly as expected have to be remaindered. It is always worth checking to see if there is something worth buying.

So much for general research. What about the heart of cookery writing, the recipes?

Organising recipe work

Recipes are the life-blood of cookery writers. Most of us start out with a notebook or looseleaf book filled with copies of recipes we have taken from friends, relations, articles and books.

Using these can cause problems. The subjects of copyright and plagiarism are covered in Chapter Eight and, for the moment, it is enough to say that you should mark details of the source of every recipe you are given, or which you cut from a magazine or newspaper or copy from a book. Note author, publisher and the date of any journal. If a friend gives you one, note the friend's name, the date and also, if they can remember, where they got it from.

When you start creating your own recipes, identify them as such, with the date, plus the details of any recipe you may have based it on.

Other aspects that need consideration when dealing with recipes are:

- Recipe storage
- Cook's notebook
- Recipe testing

Recipe storage

A few dozen recipes are not difficult to organise, but several hundred start to pose problems and some writers have thousands. It's a good idea to work out a system of filing them early on which you feel comfortable with.

If you use a word processor, it is easy to keep up-to-date master copies of recipes. If you don't have a processor or computer, there are other solutions: writing them into a notebook, filing them in a ring binder, using index cards. The important factor to remember is that you *must* be able to find whatever recipe you want easily. In Chapter Seven, various systems for organising recipes in a cookery book are discussed. One of these may well work for your personal collection as well.

Make sure that your recipes remain easily decipherable. If you note down changes, ensure that these are legible and that there is no ambiguity. If necessary, copy the new version out again.

Cook's notebook

Keep a cookery notebook in the kitchen. It's not only formal cookery sessions which produce new recipes. Sometimes using up odd ingredients in the fridge and larder to provide a simple meal can produce a particularly good result. If you haven't noted down ingredients and amounts as you work, you may not be able to remember exactly how you made the dish.

Or you may be in a hurry, throwing ingredients together, and find yourself suddenly inspired to try something that, again, works out spectacularly well, giving you a new recipe. Like a scientist, you need to make sure that you can recreate your experiments. Don't slosh in the wine. Measure it out so you know exactly how much you've used. Then note it down.

In the notebook, as well as ingredients, with amounts, and brief notes on method, add a few words giving your opinion of the dish – not only whether you liked it or not, but suggestions for its improvement. A little more of that, or less of the other. A change of ingredient, a different method. You may not want to work on it now but later your notes could provide the basis for a successful new dish. The polishing can be done when convenient.

A well-kept cookery notebook provides seed corn for future recipe creation.

Recipe testing

Never, ever, publish a recipe that hasn't been tested.

Ideally, cook every recipe from the finished version, so you know that the quantities, ingredients and method are all accurate and easy to follow.

As you test your recipe, always note changes and adjustments on your master copy as you make them. It's easy at the time to think you will remember changing three teaspoons of a strong spice to two but if you then have a difficult time with a number of similar recipes, you may well forget wanting to change the amount or be unable to remember exactly what you decided, and include the wrong information in your article or book. A good way of keeping track of changes is to date the original recipe and then to add the dates of any amendments.

Accounts

You need to organise some way of keeping track of all your expenses, some of which you should be able to offset against your income from writing. I propose to deal with this subject very briefly, as there are a number of books giving good advice which can be consulted.

If you work with a personal computer, a spreadsheet programme can solve a lot of the donkey work but I have many friends who prefer to work with an ordinary accounts book with several columns. Expenses are entered every week or month in a single column, and then analysed under different headings: post, travel, stationery, food, etc. Income should be noted in a separate column. Usually, no analysis is necessary.

Always keep supporting invoices and receipts. A ring binder or series of plastic folders can make sure they're kept tidily, or just slip them in a file.

Telephone accounts should also be kept, a proportion of which is usually allowable against income.

If you run a car, keep a log with a note of all your mileage, including non-business use. This will mean you are able to claim for a proportion of your driving expenses.

The difficulty in working with food is persuading the Inland Revenue that ingredients are allowable against income, even though your family has eaten them for supper! Keep copies of articles and books that have been published, together with itemised costs of testing the recipes, plus travel expenses involved in buying the ingredients. If the inspector starts quibbling, it can help to point out that some recipes are tested several times but not charged more than once.

Restaurant bills are even more difficult. Entertainment is not an allowable expense against tax and inspectors can have a cynical attitude towards claims that the meal was research.

Again, keep full details of who you've eaten with, together with a note of the purpose of the meal.

The cost of trips abroad can be allowable against income if they have been undertaken solely for business or the purposes of research, etc., but tagging a holiday on the end may mean you will not be able to charge anything.

If your tax office is reasonably near, it can be helpful to request an interview with the inspector handling your return. Tax officers are human beings and are usually very happy to sort out any difficulties with you, particularly after you've convinced them you have no intention of defrauding the Inland Revenue. Even a telephone call may be able to put you on the right lines.

Looking to the future

You may not need them at the moment but two items you should be thinking about are notepaper and scrapbooks.

Headed paper needn't be elaborate but should give your name as well as your address to make it look professional. I had a very simple heading designed. My address, telephone and fax number are centred under this.

As soon as you start having articles published, you should collect them in a scrapbook, or in open-topped plastic folders secured in a ring binder. They are useful for reference purposes, to have copied as examples of your published work – and to give you encouragement when you are feeling down.

Janet Laurence   Cookery

3

WRITING RECIPE BASED ARTICLES

For keen cooks, writing about food almost always means using recipes. The recipe based article is perhaps one of the easiest ways to start writing about cookery. This is because there is a demand for such articles and because their structure means the writer's mind has to focus on the two most important aspects of food and cookery writing: making the business of eating interesting and putting over recipes.

We've all read these articles. Each starts with a section dealing with a particular theme and then leads into a number of recipes. Sometimes there are little explanatory pieces or comments between the recipes. The length of the article will vary from publication to publication. Sometimes it will be very short, no more than, say, 500 words, including the recipes. In a glossy magazine it will be much longer.

There is a demand for these articles because newspapers and magazines are well aware that nearly all of us are looking for new ideas to feed ourselves, our families and friends. A lively cookery section is one way of creating readership loyalty.

A number of publications have resident cookery experts who write a regular column but there are many openings for freelances. Some publications include additional columns beside that of their resident expert, while others rely on a variety of contributors and are constantly on the look out for fresh material.

So, how do you start? Let us begin by considering first the most important part of the article: the recipes.

Recipes

The first requirement for cookery articles is original recipes that both taste and look good. Cooks who can create exciting new recipes are much rarer than writers who can handle words. One leading food editor says that 90 per cent of his commissions are for recipes.

Whatever publication you are writing for, your recipes should strive to be different from those being offered by other writers. This doesn't necessarily mean getting away from traditional dishes. Unearthing treasures from the past has yielded dividends for many a cookery writer. But if it is something very familiar, it needs a new twist or an emphasis on technique. Everyone knows about Yorkshire Pudding but there are many people who can't produce a successful one. So emphasising the secrets of a triumphal Yorkshire Pud could justify its inclusion in an article. Apple Pie can be a cliché but not if it has an unfamiliar ingredient or a new presentation.

Study recipes in newspapers and magazines. Note new twists, register original approaches and see how writers put together recipes from different parts of the world. Look at photographs, and at the way new presentational ideas give a dish interest.

The nuts and bolts of recipe writing itself are dealt with in Chapter Seven – and that chapter needs to be read in conjunction with this one before preparing an article.

Plagiarism is a charge often levelled at cookery writers and Chapter Eight deals with recipe copyright, how to avoid being accused of plagiarism and what is justified in preparing recipes for publication and what is not. What you should always strive for, though, is to create original recipes.

I am sometimes asked whether I work out new recipes for an article or book or do I already have lots that I can choose from?

Every cookery writer works in a very personal way. Some have a large selection of recipes they have created at various times, just waiting to be used. Others work them out specially, using the pressure of a deadline to provide the inspirational hothouse. I think most, though, use a combination of both. Certainly, I do. However many good recipes I've got on hand, sometimes I need to create a very specific recipe, perhaps using special ingredients or a particular technique, perhaps because I'm inspired in some way or perhaps because I feel a new approach is needed.

For the cookery writer, particularly of articles, has to be aware that cookery is as susceptible to fashion as any other aspect of life.

Ten years ago, food magazines catered for the hostess who wanted to prepare food for her dinner party that couldn't be distinguished from that offered by top chefs. If your food looked as though Anton Mosimann was lurking in the kitchen, it was reckoned a success. The criteria today are very different and magazines reflect this.

Apart from styles, different cuisines come in and go out of fashion. As I write, Italian food is all the rage. Pick up any magazine or newspaper and you will find recipes for pasta dishes and other Italian specialities. The Italian dessert Tiramisu appears on countless menus and is the new favourite with a whole host of hostesses. But, already, versions can be spotted in supermarket deep freezes, a sure sign that a dish is on the way out as far as food fashion is concerned. By the time this book appears, not only Tiramisu but the whole Italian phase may well be long gone and editors looking for something different.

Other dishes have suffered the way Tiramisu appears bound. A couple of years ago, variations on mashed potato enjoyed a brief vogue. Lentils have enjoyed a more lasting popularity. Not just any lentils, either; the truly fashionable cook has to use those from Puy in France. These are small, dark lentils that have a subtle flavour and cook quickly to a tender texture while retaining their shape.

The trick is to anticipate these fashions and be in there at the start, creating recipes that reflect the new wave in food fashions. But how does a particular cuisine or dish achieve such tremendous acceptance?

27

It's usually a combination of circumstances. One of the reasons for the recent popularity of Italian food has been the medical identification of the 'Mediterranean diet' as particularly healthy. At the same time, Great Britain went into recession and Italian food presented many economic dishes. Pasta dishes can not only be cheap but also extremely quick to prepare, which suited busy people trying to hold down a much-needed job as well as look after the family. As well, public imagination has been fired by brilliant Italian cookery writers. Marcella Hazan, an Italian cookery teacher living much of the time in the U.S., started the inspirational process and was followed by our own Anna del Conte, another writer who has achieved classic status, and the process was accelerated by a mouth-watering series of BBC television programmes presented by Valentina Harris.

It is up to you to sort out the signals that could indicate where the spotlight will fall next . . .

Early pointers can often be picked up from top chefs, both here and abroad. Putting eating down to research is a marvellous excuse for spending money in good restaurants and you may even be able to persuade the Inland Revenue to accept the bill against tax. You don't always have to eat at a restaurant, though, to pick up ideas. Read restaurant columns in the newspapers, talk to any friends who eat out at really good restaurants; new themes will soon start to identify themselves.

You probably have a whole file of splendid recipes which you are longing to incorporate into various articles. That's great. You may even have identified a possible market for which you feel you could write successfully. Even better. However, before you assemble your choicest recipes or start putting pen to paper, you need to consider the following:

- Market
- Style and approach
- Theme

Market

The market for which you are writing your article needs very careful consideration. 'Market' here is both the publication you are going to send your article to and its readership.

First, what sort of publication is likely to consider your work? The best advice to beginners is not to start with national newspapers and glossy magazines, where the competition is fierce and editors look for more than good ideas and interesting recipes. Many of them, as well, don't accept unsolicited manuscripts, the freelance contributions they use are commissioned from established writers.

There are, though, top magazines and newspapers that print recipes from readers, sometimes paying for them, other times offering a prize in kind, a bottle of champagne, say, or one of virgin olive oil. Regularly contributing recipes will sharpen your appreciation of the sort of approach which that particular publication is interested in and may also get your name known to the editor, even if the recipes aren't used. If your recipes are printed, you may be able to follow this success up by suggesting an article.

The best targets for the beginner are publications with a more restricted readership. Local newspapers and magazines are sometimes happy to receive cookery contributions. The pay won't be high but the experience will be invaluable and appearing in print means you can start a cuttings file and have published work to show other editors.

For other possibilities, research along the shelves of the largest newsagents you can find. Flip through their magazines and find which ones print cookery, then try and work out if they have a regular cookery correspondent or whether they accept work from freelances. Checking the list of editorial names will often identify a food or cookery editor or correspondent. Reading three or four issues of the same magazine will show which writers appear regularly.

Even a good newsagent won't stock every magazine that's published. Visit the library and check through press guides for more possibilities. The *Writers' and Artists' Year Book*, and *The Writer's Handbook* (*see* Appendix) give details of all the major newspapers and magazines. These include information on whether unsolicited manuscripts are welcome, if a letter proposing an idea should be sent in advance of an article and, sometimes, give guidance on how much the publication will pay. There are others, such as *Willings Press Guide*, which are even more comprehensive at covering the market. Read Chapter Six.

Style and approach

Once you have identified a market, you need to study it carefully. Each of us writes in our own particular way and personal style should be part of the charm of any article or book. It is usually possible, though, to adapt the way we write to certain requirements.

Popular journals usually want lively articles that are practical, written in a pithy style that uses short sentences and avoids long words, and with recipes that don't contain lots of ingredients, particularly expensive ones, or advanced techniques. Quite often, the articles they publish concentrate on the recipes, keeping introductions and preambles to a minimum. Upmarket journals will look for interesting introductions, a greater depth to the writing, and more unusual recipes.

The technique of actually writing articles is the same for cookery as for any other subject. Some guidance is given in Chapter Five. Read that. If you are a beginner, there are some excellent books on the market devoted entirely to writing that can be most helpful, many in this series.

Study published articles, particularly those written by the occasional freelance writers rather than regular contributors, and absorb the various techniques. Learn to identify styles and which sort of style suits which publication.

Having identified your targets and their house style, you have to angle your approach to the readership of the publication you are writing for.

Try to put yourself in the shoes of the reader of each journal you are considering as a possible market for your work. What sort of a person is he, and what does he require from this publication? Flip through several recent copies of the magazine or newspaper, and read through not only the food sections but other sections as well. Don't forget the advertising, for through it you will learn what the readership expects.

Some angles are easy to pick up. Readers of an angling magazine, for instance, are interested in fish and any cookery article that might be included will have to feature fish recipes. But there are other, more subtle indicators. Does the reader like complicated ideas, and will he appreciate depth of research? Is he prepared to spend money? Or is he looking for simple ideas that won't cost too much? Will the reader go for the quick and easy recipe or is he prepared to invest time if not money?

When I was writing for the *Daily Telegraph*, I learned that readers wanted dishes that wouldn't prove too expensive and take too much time to do but offered them something a little different. Some readers were adventurous; many had families; most liked entertaining, often just a few friends but sometimes in large numbers; and many lived in the country where some ingredients could be difficult to find but others could be anxious to try anything new. I tried to address all of these requirements in my recipes though not, of course, in every article.

An approach that can work very well with some magazines, particularly those that don't have their own kitchens, is to team up with a food photographer. You write the article, prepare and present the food while the photographer takes the pictures. You can then offer an editor an illustrated article, which means saving him the trouble of organising photography, hiring a stylist and choosing props. Have a look at Chapter Nine and remember that photographs have to be slanted towards a publication's need as accurately as an article.

The last facet to be considered is one that writers often turn to first, and that is the theme of the article.

Theme

Every article has to have a theme, which must not be confused with a basic idea.

You might think that children's birthday parties could form the basis of a good article. Perhaps you have considerable experience in catering for them and know lots of good recipes loved by children. Rather than jotting down a number of random thoughts on these parties and assembling a few wonderful recipes, it is better to consider first a theme for such an article. For a witches' and wizards' party, for instance, with decor and food to match, the recipes could provide imaginative ways of creating eye of newt and toe of frog, lizard's leg and howlet's wing, etc.

It is the theme and the idea together that will make the editor take more than the most cursory of looks at your article.

If your recipes are really original and attractive, a theme needn't be complicated. 'The Art of the Tart' is a catchy headline I remember from an article that looked at unusual recipes for both sweet and savoury tarts and quiches for a popular food magazine. Another way of looking at much the same idea for a rather different market might be to ask: 'What makes a Quiche?' and then, briefly, to explore the historical origins of the quiche in Lorraine. You will thus provide a satisfactory definition as a lead-in to your original and, preferably, unusual recipes.

Themes also enable readers to know what you are offering them. Many will be seeking inspiration for supper or the weekend's meals, while others may just like reading about food. All of them, however, want to have their minds focused on the subject of the article. So, whatever your theme, it needs to be both attractive and easily identifiable and you need to structure your article very tightly around it.

Remember that, sometimes, a short series of related articles may suit a publication. It doesn't always work but, when, it does, you've sold several articles at once and selling is often harder work than writing.

Most theme ideas fall into one of a number of easily identifiable categories. Here are a few of the more obvious:

- Personal experience
- Ingredients
- Special events
- Foreign food
- Seasonal
- Special techniques

Personal experience
Articles based on personal experience almost always manage to sound fresh because your experience is usually different from anybody else's (if it isn't, forget about it). Experiences don't always have to be successful ones. Everyone likes to read of disasters happening to someone else, particularly if, at the same time, they learn how to avoid them themselves, as the cook shows how complete catastrophe was averted.

We all face problems in the kitchen and, often, finding a solution can provide the basis for an article: unexpected guests who need feeding from a larder; having to dream up nutritious and tempting dishes for someone on a special diet; teaching children to cook from safe and interesting recipes; getting faddy children to expand their range of acceptable foods; or preparing interesting meals that require no last-minute attention.

Or, perhaps, you enjoy finding unusual ingredients and exploring their possibilities, or are inspired by a particular cook or dish. Have you discovered new recipes on a holiday abroad? There is nothing like personal experience and enthusiasm for providing a liveliness and intimacy that can establish an immediate bond with the reader – and the editor who first reads your article.

Make sure your recipes match your enthusiasm. Personal experience should mean very personal recipes.

Ingredients
Ingredients form one of the most popular categories for recipe based articles. The specialist ingredient can be anything from

abalone to zucchini. It doesn't have to be rare or expensive, more mundane items such as parsnip or parsley can produce interesting and attractive articles. If you choose ingredients you particularly like, it is easy to get enthusiastic about cooking with them and to convey this to the reader.

It's important that each recipe you create illustrates a different aspect of your chosen ingredient so that your reader gets an idea of its versatility. Using different ethnic approaches can be interesting and the historical aspect can also produce attractive angles.

Special events

Nearly everybody has to cater for certain special events: children's birthday parties; silver and golden weddings; a dinner party; a teenage rave; a buffet party. These and other occasions keep cropping up and readers are always wanting advice and new ideas for providing enjoyable food, particularly if it is quick and easy to prepare.

The trick, when using such events as the basis for an article, is to find new ideas. Use your own celebrations as spurs to create new dishes and take notes on all aspects of such occasions. Remember that the accompanying photograph for such an article will almost certainly show a tempting spread of food rather than the odd dish and your recipes should look good together.

Foreign food

Almost certainly, this is one of the easiest of themes to sell if you can write with some depth of knowledge.

The days are gone when readers could be satisfied with a cookery writer's experiences based on two weeks of eating in restaurants in a foreign country. Today, you need to write with a genuine understanding of a country's cuisine and the culture that has produced it. You need to know which are the most popular dishes, how the food can vary from region to region, and which are the indigenous ingredients that make it what it is.

Particularly important, when writing of foreign food, is an

ability to convey taste and texture to someone who may never have come across the sort of dish you are describing. When you are abroad, always practise describing the new food you are eating. Gradually extending your knowledge of a particular country's food will bring nearer the day when you feel competent to write an article on it.

Clare Ferguson is a cookery writer who does a lot of travelling and is always trying new dishes. As soon as she gets home, she works at recreating the ones she has enjoyed. When she thinks she has a dish more or less right, she will try to find a local recipe to see if she can learn more about it and improve her method.

Remember that articles based on foreign food often need an additional theme to make them acceptable. 'Food from Sweden' will probably be too vague, while 'Successful Smorgasbord Suppers' might find a home.

Seasonal

Warming winter food, summer *al fresco* food, Hallowe'en, Christmas and Easter celebrations, self-catering holidays, seasonal foods (especially from the garden); all these and many more can be used as the basis of an article – and are every year. They will continue to inspire yet more articles because they fulfil a continuing need. Readers who are new to cooking need guidance, and experienced readers look for something different or variations on the dishes they have been producing for years.

This category might seem to offer easy choices for beginners but there are difficulties for freelances.

Seasonal articles, by their very nature, can only be used at one particular time of the year. Submitting this sort of article needs careful timing. Both daily and weekly newspapers make initial decisions on the content of a features page several weeks before publication day. Monthly and even weekly magazines work much farther ahead. They sometimes require copy several months before the issue reaches the news-stands and decisions on the content of particular issues will have been made several weeks earlier than that. If you have an article suitable for a magazine's Christmas issue, June or July is not too early to send it in for consideration.

Because you have to work far ahead, it's sometimes impossible to get hold of the right ingredients to work out recipes. Always try to work with seasonal items when they are freely available. Even if you have no immediate use for the recipes, once you have created successful ones, you can be sure that the right home for them will soon crop up.

The second difficulty with this sort of article as far as freelances are concerned, is that writers with regular columns often structure their pieces round such seasonal themes. Any other articles used in the same publication usually have to have a rather different theme.

Special techniques
If you thoroughly understand cookery processes, then a successful theme can be based around showing the average reader how to tackle an advanced technique, either through one or a number of affiliated recipes. How to produce a successful soufflé, for instance, or puff pastry.

The market for this sort of article, however, is not as wide as for other themes, since, usually, only magazines specialising in food will be interested. It is also a theme that is more difficult to adapt to a variety of approaches and, once a magazine has covered a particular technique, it is not likely to want another article on it for some considerable time.

You may well be able to think of other sorts of themes. Chapter Four explores the various categories cookery books fall into and that may give you more ideas for articles.

4

WRITING COOKERY BOOKS

Most of us have a precious collection of recipes we feel would make a wonderful cookery book. After all, they are always successful; you and your family love them, so why shouldn't other people? Isn't everybody always looking for something new, something different? Why shouldn't our well-loved dishes provide the answer?

Maybe your recipes are already written into a manuscript book or are assembled in some sort of binder; they will be dog-eared and fat-splashed, covered with notations and suggestions – true – but everything is there. Perhaps there's an amusing story or two that can be worked in, or maybe you have already made some notes for graceful introductions. Surely all it needs is a grand organisation and typing session and the whole thing can be sent off to some lucky publisher?

If it is this sort of dream that started you reading this book, prepare yourself to shake up your ideas. There will need to be a great deal of thought and hard work before you are ready to approach a publisher.

A competitive field

Go into any decent-sized book shop and you will find a considerable proportion of shelf space devoted to books on cookery and food. So you could be forgiven for thinking that this is an easy area to break into. Be warned, it is not! The competition is fierce and many of the books published make very little, if any, money.

There is no need to get too despondent, though. Publishers do want cookery books. In fact, they are so anxious to find successful ideas, they are willing to give serious consideration to submissions from unpublished writers. But what they are looking for are books that will sell. It's no use approaching them with your dog-eared collection of recipes, however nicely you've typed them out.

You need to think very carefully about exactly what sort of cookery book you are going to write. You need to think about your strengths and weaknesses, where your experience lies and what the market lacks. And you need to think about what a publisher is looking for. Let's start with that.

What a publisher looks for

There are three main criteria any publisher will expect a cookery book to meet:

- Originality of approach
- Expertise
- Ability to meet a market need

Originality of approach
This means, quite simply, that your book has to be different from anybody else's.

In 1985, *Grub on a Grant* (Headline) by Cas Clarke was published. Cas Clarke was not a cook and had no ambitions to be a cookery writer, but she had just graduated from Sussex University and thought that her experiences feeding herself and her friends could help other students. So she put together a short book filled with cheap and cheerful dishes, plus the odd one, like a roast, that was more expensive – none of them very original. Written in a bright and breezy style, with lots of useful tips for the student cook, it is still in print, having changed publishers, and continues to sell steadily. It has become as much of a classic as Katherine

Whitehorn's *Cooking in a Bedsit* (Penguin), which was written a generation earlier.

Grub on a Grant, and, indeed, *Cooking in a Bedsit*, succeeded because the basic idea was fresh and original, the treatment suited the idea and there was a market eager for the book.

The Legendary Cuisine of Persia (Lieuse Publications), by Margaret Shaida, won the Glenfiddich Food Book of the Year Award in 1993. Once again, Margaret Shaida was not a cookery writer and here, again, was an idea for a book that filled a niche in the market. Margaret Shaida, though, had great difficulty in finding a publisher; she was told that her book, attractive though it was, would be too expensive to produce and the market for it was too limited. In the end she took a brave step and published it herself.

These two stories show that, in the main, the ideas that publishers welcome most from new writers are those that are cheap to produce and will appeal to a wide audience.

So choose an idea that will attract a large market, that hasn't already been done and won't be too expensive. If you can think of a clever title as well, your book will need little selling.

Expertise

If you are thinking of writing a cookery book, you must be a good cook. You don't, however, have to have taken a *cordon bleu* course or be able to produce certificates to prove your ability.

Cas Clarke had no cooking expertise to offer beyond her experience as a student. But it is perfectly obvious, as you read *Grub on a Grant*, that she knows exactly what she is writing about. Her instructions, which are short and to the point, are what the student working from her book will understand and have confidence in. That is what publishers will be looking for in your book: the confidence that you understand what you are writing about. Flourish qualifications if you have them, as they may well be helpful, but what a good editor trusts is his instinct as he reads your manuscript. Sometimes, though, an editor will give your book to an experienced cook and ask for their opinion, and maybe ask them to try some of the recipes.

Ability to meet a market need

The final criterion publishers look for is ability to meet a market need. Your recipes may be excellent and your writing original, but if the subject is one already well covered or so abstruse no one will be interested in it, the book will be difficult to sell to a publisher. Having assessed the market possibilities for your book, do some research to make sure someone else hasn't already produced the definitive volume on the subject.

Go to the largest book shop you can find and start checking along the shelves. Even better, if you are in London, visit *Books for Cooks* (see Appendix) who are the largest U.K. retailers of cookery books. The shop is often approached by publishers wanting to check what gaps exist in the cookery book market that they may be able to fill.

U.S.P. and you

The Unique Selling Proposition is an old marketing term and one that it is useful to remember when trying to assess how your book will be welcomed by a publisher. A book is a product like any other and it is its U.S.P. that will sell it to a publisher and, ultimately, the reader.

It is sensible, when searching for an idea with U.S.P., to look first at yourself rather than at the market. Very often you can find that you already have a specialist area of knowledge waiting to be tapped. Sometimes, all it needs is to be angled in a particular way to make it acceptable to a publisher.

When my husband retired, I faced the problem of providing meals every day for the two of us. We no longer entertained very often so there were few 'left-overs' to help out. Recipes for four often proved difficult to halve – what do you do when the result calls for half an egg? And what happens to that left-over piece of aubergine? One day, as I was wondering what to do with a couple of lamb chops to make them a little different, it occurred to me there must be whole armies of cooks faced with the same problem. Not only women with retired husbands, but those whose families had left home, couples sharing flats, newly-weds, or people living on their own who liked to have just one other person round for a meal. I couldn't think of any book currently on the market that met these needs.

I realised that here was a perfect subject for a cookery book and one that I was well qualified to write. It would be rooted in my own experience, which is always the best background for a book. I couldn't wait to get lunch over so I could start on the outline. A couple of years later, *Just for Two* was published by Hodder & Stoughton.

Margaret Shaida wrote *The Legendary Cuisine of Persia* after she spent 25 years living in Iran with her husband. On their return to England, she started cooking Persian food for English friends and found not only that they loved it but that they wanted to find out more about its background and how to cook it. There were no books she could recommend – until she wrote one. Here, again, was a subject that offered itself to an author equipped with the necessary experience and knowledge to write the book.

What about you? You may well have an area of your life that offers similarly valuable experience. It might be that you have an ethnic background that has instilled a deep knowledge of another country's culinary heritage (some foreign countries are difficult, though. Unless you can develop a very unusual angle, you would have problems selling a book on French or Italian cooking, for instance, since the market is already saturated).

Maybe you have been cooking with a physical disability. Or have spent years doing self-catering holidays or cooking on a boat, learning how to deal with shopping for food in a foreign language, cooking with unfamiliar ingredients and coping with minimal equipment. Perhaps you are very successful at teaching children how to cook, knowing what they can absorb, what excites them and how ambitious they can be. You may have had to cope with dietary problems and found very little on the bookshelves to help you. There are, in fact, all sorts of experiences that could equip you to write a cookery book.

Perhaps, however, there isn't any personal experience you can identify. Don't despair. Look, instead, at your particular strengths. Do you like research? There are books waiting to be written around information to be found in libraries and other sources. Are you good at talking to people and drawing them out? Their cooking experiences may be able to provide you with some valuable ideas. Do you love playing about with unusual ingredients in the kitchen? You may be able to help others anxious to cook with them as well. It is possible, in fact, to start from scratch with a basic idea and turn it into a book.

Financial specialist, Jim Slater, has evolved what he calls the 'Zulu principle'. His theory goes something like this: if you choose a little-known area of knowledge and follow it through, it doesn't take very long before you become a leading expert. Success, though, says Mr Slater, depends not only on finding a little-known subject but identifying it as one which other people can be interested in and then being able to maximise its potential.

Choosing your subject

Ideas for cookery books fall into categories, and not every category calls for the same talents. It is important, therefore, to be realistic about your particular abilities and to recognise what sort of idea you have come up with. Most cookery books will fit into one of the following categories:

Single ingredient or product
These books are the antithesis of the 'general' book. They

take a single subject and cover it exhaustively. Titles such as Lindsey Bareham's *In Praise of the Potato* (Grafton) and Anne Dolamore's *The Essential Olive Oil Companion* (Macmillan) fall into this category. You need a deep and genuine interest in your chosen subject and an ability to approach it from every angle, including the unexpected. You must be willing to research your ingredient or product's history, cultivation, culture and a wide variety of recipes that include it. At the end of writing such a book your family and friends may never want to eat potatoes, chocolate or peanuts again but you should only require the shortest of pauses before looking for yet another way of cooking with them. A dedicated enthusiast can approach a subject like this with little prior knowledge and turn it into a triumphant success through hard work and imagination.

Thematic
Much the same as above except that the subject matter is rather more widely based. It could be a type of food, such as Jane Grigson's *Charcuterie and French Pork Cookery* (Penguin), or regional, or be all embracing, like Margaret Costa's classic *Four Seasons Cookbook* (Sphere). Thematic books need an ability to identify the details that make your subject special, plus all the requirements mentioned above.

Occasions
This is a variation on the 'theme' category. Books can be written catering for particular occasions: picnics, parties, self-catering, sailing, etc. There is scope here for a very individual approach. Success depends, in part, on choosing an occasion that is attractive to a sufficiently wide market. Golden weddings might make a good subject for an article but the audience could be considered a little small for a book. Widen it to all sorts of wedding celebrations and you might be in business.

Ethnic
Sometimes a holiday abroad can inspire an urge to expand traditional dishes, sampled under a sunny sky, into a full

43

length book. I have to say that it almost always requires a very deep knowledge, gained over a number of years, to write successfully of a cuisine which is not your own. If, however, you find yourself based in a new country, then researching its food and traditional dishes is a highly enjoyable activity for any cook. Gilli Davies was already a food and cookery writer when her army husband was stationed in Cyprus and she lost no time in learning not only about Cypriot food but its culture and history. She was finally able to produce *The Taste of Cyprus – A Seasonal Look at Cypriot Cooking* (Interworld).

Culinary/dietary

Here, we are looking at a particular approach to eating: vegetarianism, cooking for an allergy, slimming, etc. These books are best written from a personal viewpoint. There have been spectacularly successful slimming books, almost always written by someone who has discovered a dietary approach that works particularly well for them. Rosemary Conley's *Hip and Thigh Diet* (Arrow) is one that springs to mind. Books written from a more theoretical approach seldom catch on in the same way; it seems as though personal enthusiasm is necessary. One of our most successful vegetarian writers is Colin Spencer, who admits to eating fish and game occasionally but is passionate about animal well-being. That dedication gives him a commitment to making vegetarian food delicious that has enabled him to produce many delightful cookery books for the non-meat eater.

Explanatory

These are 'how to' books which can deal with anything from the master class approach through cooking for the physically disabled to dealing with unusual foods. 'Master class' books need to be written by someone who understands the theory of basic principles and has usually taught the subject, thereby gaining an appreciation of how the inexperienced may fall foul of various points. Unusual foods need to be experimented with and traditional ways of using them looked at, as well as more novel approaches.

Equipment based

There are items of equipment that raise a need for books exploring their use. For instance, the chicken brick, food processor, wok, etc. Ever since microwave ovens reached the mass market there has been a constant stream of books addressing the problem of fulfilling their potential in the home kitchen. It might be thought that every possible approach had been covered, but a few years ago Barbara Kafka enjoyed a huge success with the *Microwave Gourmet* (Headline), which was the result of considerable research into an often revolutionary way of microwave cooking. Sometimes, a traditional cooking utensil can be given a new lease of life by culinary fashion, often stimulated by a television series. Chinese cooking and the wok is an example of this. It's an area where you need a good eye for seeing new potential or are already working in an area that brings new cookery equipment to your attention.

Historical

Interest in the cooking of all our yesterdays has grown greatly over the last decade or so and a number of authors have trawled through old cookery books and manuscripts for interesting recipes that can be enjoyed today. Some include a commentary on their background. One of the best of these is *Elinor Fettiplace's Receipt Book* (Viking/Salamander) by Hilary Spurling, based on a manuscript recipe book (dated 1604) inherited by her husband. After some ten years spent cooking many of the recipes, Hilary Spurling, a biographer, critic and literary editor, decided to try to interest a publisher in the MS together with a carefully researched and attractively written account of food, cooking and eating in Elizabethan times. It is successful because not only is the author extremely talented both as a cook and writer, but she also understands historical disciplines.

Personal choice

This constitutes general dishes put together by the author without any particular theme. Jane Grigson's *Good Things*

(Penguin), a charming selection of enjoyable dishes, is an excellent example. As mentioned earlier, these books are very hard to sell to a publisher unless you have a well-known name or can claim first-class professional qualifications, such as that of a leading chef or head of a cookery school. If you are a desk top publisher, however, a short collection could make a delightful present for a child or friends, see Chapter Eleven.

Collections
This includes recipes donated by the famous or those belonging to a particular group of people, such as Royal Academicians or members of a particular association or society. Usually, such a collection is sold in aid of some cause or charity. These books seem simple since all that appears to be required is the ability to charm sufficient recipes from your chosen group of people to make up the size of book you want. However, it needs considerable organisational talent – plus the skill to edit very different contributions into a coherent style. Such collections need a really original basic idea to make them acceptable to a commercial publisher. One such was *Last Suppers* (Nadder Books), a book that consisted of a number of leading chef's recipes for their choice of their last meal on earth, compiled by Jeremy Gunn. In the main, though, this sort of book is best looked on as a fund-raising project.

Defining your approach

Along with identifying the subject of your book, you also need to think about how you will write it and how you would like it to look. The nuts and bolts of how to write recipes and organise them into a book are discussed in Chapter Seven but you need also to think about the various styles in which your book can be written. Most cookery books are more than a simple stringing together of recipes with the odd introduction. Here's a list of different approaches with a brief description of each:

- Minimalist
- Anecdotal/autobiographical
- Intellectual
- Technical
- Humorous
- Illustrative

Minimalist

The minimalist approach sets out recipes as clearly as possible and gives no more than a few words of introduction. In order for this style to be successful, the recipes have to be original and exciting. You see it most often used for the collections of great chefs. Today, however, even many of them feel the need to add anecdotes, background, or some attractive detail that brings a recipe to life.

Anecdotal/autobiographical

This style of writing is suited to a wide range of books. The recipes are accompanied by stories that illustrate and enliven their background. These can be garnered from a wide range of sources: where the dish was first eaten, an amusing story connected with it, some detail surrounding a particular ingredient, a point of technique that will ensure its success, or perhaps the recipe's place in the author's life.

Occasionally, such a book can be called autobiographical. The 1991 Glenfiddich Food Book of the Year was *Memories of Gascony* (Headline), by Pierre Koffmann, written with Timothy Shaw, in which the chef patron of London's *Tante Claire* restaurant set his recipes, like polished jewels, into a wonderfully detailed account of growing up on a farm in Gascony with its rich food tradition.

In fact, so vibrant is Koffman's account, it borders on the next approach.

Intellectual

Here the author accompanies detailed background information with historical and cultural insights into the book's recipes, thus expanding the reader's appreciation of the dishes.

The intellectual approach is more and more popular these days, for it talks to intelligent readers who look for more from a recipe book than a mere dish to cook. An unexpected success a few years ago was Patience Gray's *Honey From a Weed – Fasting and Feasting in Tuscany, Catalonia, the Cyclades and Apulia* (Prospect Books) which is based on the author's experiences of living and cooking in primitive conditions in various Mediterranean locations. The book's title gives some idea of its scholarship but little of its humour, wide-ranging knowledge, the approachability of its writing and the practicality of the recipes. It is an exceptional book.

Technical
With this approach, the writing is geared principally towards 'how to'. This could be concerned with cooking techniques or a particular food style, such as how to cut out carbohydrates or avoid wheat, or how to deal with particular ingredients. It concentrates on the nuts and bolts, both practical and theoretical. *Queer Gear – How to Buy and Cook Exotic Fruits and Vegetables* (Century Hutchinson), by Carolyn Heal and Michael Allsop, concentrates on all you need to know about those sometimes strange-looking items that crop up in supermarkets or ethnic greengrocers. It is packed with all sorts of interesting information.

Humorous
Different, again, is the humorous approach. Often combined with a blunt and forthright way of dealing with cookery, it can inspire confidence in the most hopeless of cooks. *Grub on a Grant* by Cas Clarke is an apt example of this. but don't attempt to be humorous unless it comes naturally to you! Nor is this style always appropriate. If it's well done, though, it is very attractive and, allied to suitable recipes, warmly welcomed by publishers.

Illustrative
With this, the recipes are accompanied by numerous pictures, usually photographs, showing exactly how to approach the

cooking, with the writing often kept to a minimum. Anne Willan's *Look and Cook* (Dorling Kindersley) series is a good example. Or the book might use a wealth of mouth-watering photographs which ensure it lives its life on a coffee table, rather than leaning on a kitchen shelf. Such books are normally expensive to produce and first-time writers do not find them easy to sell to publishers.

A few years ago, however, Kit Chapman, managing director of The Castle, a luxury hotel in Taunton, Somerset, owned by the Chapman family, wrote *Great British Chefs* (Pyramid Books), a book which combines excellent descriptions of some of Britain's current leading chefs, and a selection of their recipes, with beautiful photographs from Martin Brigdale. The book cost £19.95 in 1989, but, even at that price, such was its success that it went into a second edition and projected its author into two television series. Kit already had a name in the food world but he had never published a book before – one of those exceptions that prove the rule.

When considering your approach, remember some advice given by Anna Powell, Headline's editor in charge of cookery. She says, 'It is better to rely on words rather than presentation to sell your book'.

Identifying the reader

Choosing your style depends not only on your personal inclinations as a writer but also on the readership you intend to reach.

Someone who buys your book principally as a kitchen aid could find that not only is a lot of extraneous detail superfluous, but that it interferes with the way they want to use it.

Those readers, though, who declare they devour cookery books 'like novels', appreciate background information and details that expand their culinary knowledge. Their enjoyment of a recipe is enhanced when they know something of its cultural heritage or an interesting anecdote connected with it.

Another requirement is to assess what degree of technical skill your readers can be expected to possess. This will determine how much instruction they will need in basic skills and in choosing the ingredients and equipment needed to cook your dishes.

So you can see that there are a whole number of factors that need to be considered before you do so much as choose a recipe or write an introductory paragraph for your book.

To sum up, here is a useful piece of advice from a cookery editor. She says she likes authors who 'make it fun and speak with an individual voice'.

Everything in life is easier for a bit of fun and it's the lively books that are successful. Remember, also, that your book is just that, *your* book. It should reflect your personality, the way you speak and your approach to cooking. If you try to imitate someone else's style, no matter how successful you feel it is, your book will fail to come alive or do justice to your ideas and recipes. Your book needs to be as individual and personal as you can make it.

5

FOOD ARTICLES AND BOOKS

Not all food writing is recipe based. 'Food' means so much more than just cooking. It is a complex subject with many different angles and can offer fertile ground for the freelance writer.

There is a critical difference between cookery writers and food writers and also between food writers and general writers.

Cookery writers have to be technicians. They are concerned with the actual production of food in the kitchen. They may also be very talented writers, but there are many successful cookery writers who would never lay claim to any great expertise with the pen. They make their mark through their recipes. Some of them, usually guided by perceptive editors, become more than adequate writers; but the main merit of their work lies in their ability to conjure up original dishes.

With food writers, the emphasis is entirely on ideas and information – and the way that these are expressed. But it is not enough to be able to produce lively and original writing if you wish to gain a reputation as a food writer.

There are general journalists and authors who may produce articles and books on food, and very good ones, but cannot be considered as 'food writers'.

The distinguishing feature is attitude.

The food writer is *involved* with his subject. He doesn't have to be an expert cook but he should love food. For him, eating is an exciting experience. Finding out about any aspect of food should be an adventure. Visiting a new area, either at home or abroad, means an opportunity for new food experiences, unfamiliar ingredients, different retail outlets, new producers, processors or restaurants.

Eating, for the food writer, be it in a restaurant, someone else's home or just snacking, means absorbing and assessing every detail.

In a bookshop, the food writer will head first for the food and cookery section to check new publications.

In a new town, he heads for the local market and the food shops.

In the country, he looks for producers.

Abroad, he wants to seek out the local cuisine.

Having to get up early to visit a market or a baker is not a chore, it is a treat; any reluctance to get out of bed is offset by the anticipation of what lies ahead.

The food writer understands that what we eat affects and is affected by every aspect of our lives. In her award-winning book, *Much Depends on Dinner* (Penguin), anthropologist Margaret Visser takes a simple meal and looks at the various ingredients that make it up, tracing their economic, industrial, social, religious and psychological significance as well as their nutritional importance. After reading her book (and her light touch makes it a highly enjoyable experience), all food becomes charged with much more than mere gustatory significance.

The food writer, in fact, is an enthusiast for whom writing about food is writing with commitment. The variety of approaches are legion and few areas offer more choice of subject matter, but the message is always that food is important.

Food writers also realise that they bear responsibility, in that they can affect the public's perception of a particular product or process. Irradiation of food has been given such a bad press in this country by food writers, despite its being given a clean bill of health by the governmental experts, that leading retailers have refused to stock products which have been thus treated. And it is largely food writers who have been responsible for public antipathy towards battery chickens and eggs, by alerting them to the unpleasant facts.

There are many very talented food writers, and newcomers have to recognise that they are entering a very competitive field. But editors are always looking for a fresh approach and original ideas and there is no reason why beginners who recognise what the requirements are should not be successful.

So what are these requirements? What do you need beyond a deep interest in food?

Points to consider for articles

We are principally concerned in this book with the particular business of writing about food and cookery and that doesn't leave much space for dealing with writing techniques. If you are a beginner, there are a number of books on the market that can be helpful. For an excellent look at the nuts and bolts of writing any sort of article, I can recommend *The Craft of Writing Articles* by Gordon Wells, in this series.

As an introduction, or a recap, though, the main rules for writing articles are:

- Study your market
- Write for a particular publication
- Structure your article
- Be interesting
- Write to an acceptable length
- Consider possibilities for illustrations
- Be professional

Study your market
All the points made earlier on choosing possible markets for recipe based articles apply here and, if you haven't read that section already, do so. Briefly, though, you need to study up-to-date copies of magazines and newspapers and identify opportunities for freelance writers that will suit you. Study the shelves of a good newsagent then buy those publications

that seem really hopeful. Read more than one edition; that will help identify regular contributors and the opportunities for freelances. The library will yield reference books such as *Willings Press Guide* listing all U.K. publications together with a brief description of their contents. Order those that seem promising, if necessary through the subscription department (but *see* Chapter Six first).

Then analyse the publication. What is its readership? What are readers interested in? What sort of style are articles written in? How long are they?

Write for a particular publication

The way not to get published is to write an article and then start sending it off to publications you think might be interested. Articles need to be tailored to an editor's specific needs. This is where market research comes in.

Structure your article

All articles should have an opening, a main development and an ending.

The opening should be as eye-catching as possible. Your first few sentences have to command the attention not only of the editor you send it to, but also, of course, of his readers. If you can't grab them immediately, the rest of your article will go unread. Successful openings often pick out a controversial quotation or interesting idea from the main body of the article.

After the opening, the article should develop your idea or theme. Successful articles introduce novel ideas and explore them in depth. Even the cleverest ideas need to be developed and that usually entails research. Make sure your sources are up-to-date, for events in the food world can move very rapidly and what is current today may be old hat tomorrow. Don't be afraid of ringing up people who could have relevant opinions on the subject of your article. Most are delighted to be asked to comment and their views could give your article an authority – and flavour – that will pick it out from others.

The end of an article should be like the last course of a

dinner party, it should linger in the mind after the table has been left or the page turned. Make your ending positive. A pithy summing up of the situation you have been describing, a new idea to leave with the reader or maybe a question he can ponder, are all effective.

Be interesting

What keeps you reading any article? If it's a specialist article, it's the idea and the information that you're being given. Provided that the article flows nicely, you aren't bothered by the actual writing. But if the ideas aren't new, the information is out of date or you are already familiar with the arguments being put forward, your interest in the article is lost.

An article in a more general publication isn't written with the same amount of depth, because it has to appeal to a readership without a specialised background to place detail against. What keeps their interest is the quality not only of the information but how it is put over, in other words, how it is written.

All writers have to learn interesting ways of communicating their message. For most of us it's a long, hard process that involves imaginative thinking around the main idea and a great deal of rewriting and polishing. There are some writers who can make the slightest of ideas absorbing, while others have to make sure that the subject matter itself can hold the attention. To use a food analogy: superb meat can be cooked simply and you can rely on its flavour and texture for effect, but cheaper cuts need more complicated treatment to provide a satisfactory dish.

Write to an acceptable length

If your article has to be cut because it is too long, you, the writer, are very rarely given a choice over what has to go. When I was writing for the *Daily Telegraph*, I had a limited number of words, which I sometimes used to exceed – in the hope that there would be less advertising that week and that the complete article would get published. It was usually a vain hope. What the sub-editor thought should go rarely matched what I thought could be left out. I soon learned to keep to the prescribed number of words although, even then, advertising pressure meant I was sometimes cut.

If you have approached an editor and been given guidance on length, make sure your article doesn't exceed it. If you are sending in a piece 'on spec', find out what is likely to be a suitable length and write to that.

Consider possibilities for illustrations

Saving your editor trouble is a good way to endear yourself to him. If you can send suitable illustrations with your article, or details that will enable him to obtain them, you can often increase your chances of acceptance. Chapter Nine deals with possible approaches to illustrations.

Be professional

Professionalism means ensuring that your article is delivered on time, to length and properly presented (*see* Chapter Six).

Be reliable. Make sure every fact is checked and that any quotations are accurate and not liable to be challenged. An editor will nearly always prefer to commission a writer who is unexceptional but reliable and accurate, rather than one who is brilliant but liable to be late with his material and open to challenge on some of the content of his article.

Being professional also means concentrating on putting over your points succinctly. Most editors will tell you that articles from beginners usually have to be drastically cut, often by as much as fifty per cent. Instead of moving from point to point, they elaborate by saying the same thing again – in a different way. If you find that, after cutting, your article isn't long enough, it probably didn't have enough ideas and may well be unusable.

Writing books

A book, unlike an article, looks at a subject in depth, and explores all its angles. The writer can be more relaxed, not having to worry quite so much about adding sparkle. He still, though, has to grab the reader's interest at the start of his book and then hold it throughout its length.

Before embarking on a book, you should first sell the idea to a publisher. Read Chapter Six for advice on researching the market and preparing a synopsis and sample chapter.

Like an article, a book has a structure, though one that is more complicated. Preparing a synopsis identifies a book's sinews, its content, and the exposition of its arguments.

Style comes later, when you write your sample chapter. That is when you have to think not only about what you want to say, but how it is said. For a beginner the best advice is to concentrate on getting over your subject matter simply and directly. A food writer I spoke to said she tries to visualise her reader. Do the same. Identify what sort of person he is, why he wants to read your book, and then talk to him as you would if he were present in the room with you.

Possible subjects for food writing

Food writing for articles and books can be divided into various categories, each one of which calls for a slightly different approach:

- Personal experience
- News stories
- Specialist
- People
- General
- Restaurant reviews

It's not necessary to do more than give you a few pointers on each since you will be able to think of many more angles for yourselves.

Personal experience
This is the easiest category for the beginner because it usually

makes for vivid writing. You are conveying your own experiences, you know your subject intimately and often have anecdotes which help enliven your article or book.

Be careful, though. The success of *A Year in Provence* (Pan) with its deceptively easy style has led many a person to think that the world is waiting for his own version of life as he sees it. Writing this sort of book successfully is much more difficult than it seems. It is possible, though. David Atkins, a leading apple grower, has written a successful account of his experiences as an apple farmer in *The Cuckoo in June* (Dovecote Press).

Though it contains much valuable advice on apple growing, the book is a delightful read, even if you are totally uninterested in fruit farming, because of its wealth of pertinent anecdotes. By the end of the book, the reader feels that he knows not only the author, but also his family and staff, and has experienced with them their triumphs and disasters. David Atkins' talent for the telling phrase produces many happy descriptions; the Cox is referred to as 'a very difficult apple to grow. It is like a fragile English girl who can only be pollinated with tender loving care, a warm bed and gentle handling.'

Personal experience articles are easier to sell than a whole book. A crisply written account of some area of personal experience can usually find a receptive market if the experience is relevant and the publication chosen with care. Several articles can then sometimes form the basis of a book.

News stories
Newspapers and magazines are always eager for news stories and they abound in the food world. Organic farming, food processing, the marketing of food, health and safety, nutrition, new products, legislation and its effect on various areas, all these continually offer new developments and angles – and there are many more.

Once you get into the habit of exploring and writing news stories, you will find it easier and easier to discover more. If you get a name for such stories, people will start to contact you with interesting details, saving you a good deal of leg-work. As you build up background knowledge, your articles will gain in depth and authority and will be increasingly welcome.

Books that cover new developments in detail are much more difficult since the subject has to be of sufficient importance to warrant both the length and the lapse in time it takes for it to be published.

A very successful book developed from a news story is *The Food Scandal* (Century) by Caroline Walker and Geoffrey Cannon.

In July 1983, the *Sunday Times* revealed that a governmental report recommending a healthy diet had still not been published two and a half years after its submission. The NACNE (National Advisory Committee on Nutrition Education) report recommended that the average British diet needed to cut down on fat, sugar and salt; and the *Sunday Times* suggested it had been hushed up because of commercial pressures from powerful food interests.

Caroline Walker, a nutritionist and secretary of the NACNE team, along with Geoffrey Cannon, a writer with an interest in the relationship between food and health, wrote the book both to explain the report and its background and to give the ordinary person sufficient information to follow NACNE's recommendations for a healthy diet.

The book contains a wealth of information that is made easily digestible by its straightforward style. Because the report was recognised as being of fundamental importance to the health of the nation, it was still being debated by the time *The Food Scandal* was published in 1984 and the book enjoyed considerable success.

Specialist
Specialist aspects of food writing can range from the scientific to an examination of a particular food. This category can take in history, economics, social issues, technical developments, nutrition and many more along the way.

Specialist subjects need to be treated in depth and tend to

be addressed to a professional audience. It helps to be qualified in the field in which you are writing. On the other hand, scientists and technical people often find difficulty in writing for publication. *The Food Scandal*, mentioned above, could qualify as a specialist book written for a general market and it is the combination of scientific background and journalistic ability, provided by the joint authors, that makes it such a successful work.

For beginners who are prepared to undertake a lot of research, however, the specialist area could be fruitful, because it depends for its effect on the information and ideas offered, rather than on clever writing.

If you have a specialist background, try to develop news articles for publications with a particular interest in your field. There are many more writers around than specialists, and journalists who can combine the two are much sought-after. Articles interpreting technical developments for the general reader can also find a ready market.

A specialist approach to a general subject can result in a book with a long-lasting life. 1949 saw the publication of Redcliffe Salaman's *The History and Social Influence of the Potato* (Cambridge Press). The title says it all; the book ranges through anthropology, archaeology, botany, agriculture, economic and social history, and covers every aspect of this staple item. It even includes an examination of the potato in the realm of art. Though most people will find something of interest in it, it's not a book written for the general market, as its style is somewhat dry. However, its exhaustive nature has ensured the book classic status. It was reprinted in 1970, and again in 1985 with a new introduction and corrections by J. G. Hawkes.

The scope for a non specialist in this field is demonstrated by Henry Hobhouse's book, *Seeds of Change* (Sidgwick & Jackson). A journalist-turned-farmer, the author takes five basic products: cotton, sugar cane, potato, quinine and tea, and traces their effect on mankind. This stimulating book has been called the vegetable view of history and is a first-class example of how food can be seen as a vital ingredient – not only in our diet but also many other aspects of our lives.

People

Everyone loves reading about people.

Articles featuring interviews with famous names in the food world can often find a ready home if they are angled in a newsworthy way. The opening of a chef's new restaurant, the publication of a book, a new career development – all these can provide good hooks for a saleable interview.

Famous names, though, tend to employ PR people who approach journalists with an invitation for an interview. Unless he has particularly good connections, the beginner is more likely to find likely prospects amongst unknown people involved in interesting aspects of the food industry. What they are doing – and the problems they meet – can often provide an interesting article for either a specialist publication or a general one, particularly if the people involved have come from a 'non-food' background.

Biographies of historical food people, chefs, writers, farmers, scientists and others, can produce interesting books. They take, however, considerable research.

General

If you are a lively writer, there are other foodie subjects that can provide successful articles and books. Shopping is of perennial interest, and what to buy abroad or in particular regions can produce an interesting article if not a whole book. There is quite a vogue these days for guides to food producers and food shops.

Food marketing is first cousin to shopping. The retail industry, supermarkets, direct mail, and farm shops can all offer interesting stories.

Humorous pieces are very difficult to write but food offers plenty of scope on the subject, and there are many magazines and papers eager for writers who can make people laugh.

Exposé stories can also prove fruitful, as there is considerable reader interest today in accounts of adulteration, animal abuse, health risks, etc. You need to be very sure of your facts on such stories. Nothing should be taken for granted, everything should be checked and rechecked, and evidence given by others should be in writing; the costs of libel can be very high and authors can be held financially liable by publishers for libel actions arising out of their work.

Restaurant reviews
What a wonderful thought – to have meals in expensive restaurants paid for by writing about them! There are, indeed food writers who have found fame, if not fortune, in this way. Drew Smith, the current editor of *Taste* magazine, won a Glenfiddich Award for reviews he wrote while working for a regional newspaper. He was then invited to edit the *Good Food Guide* and the rest, as they say, is history.

However, these days few publications can afford to cover the kind of expenses that are required by serious restaurant reviewing. Some publications reserve this task for the editor or another favoured staff member on an expenses-only basis, treating it as a perk. There are also a handful of outside contributors writing regular reviews; most are chosen for their incisive, entertaining and contentious style or specialist knowledge. Joining these select few is a very difficult business.

If, though, you are content to pay for your meal yourself, you may well be able to interest a publication in restaurant reviews. Local papers are probably the most likely markets. The fee will almost certainly not cover the cost of your dining but if you are eating out anyway, any small contribution towards the bill could be welcome and the cutting can be added to your file.

A serious restaurant reviewer needs a very good palate, confidence in his own judgement and an in-depth knowledge of cooking. These days, restaurants tend to pride themselves on creating their own recipes rather than recreating classic dishes – but if you come across a sauce Bearnaise, for instance, you should know what it is supposed to look and taste like. You should also be able to identify when a sauce is well balanced, what the flavour and texture of well hung beef is, what the difference is between a fine extra-virgin olive oil and an ordinary one and many other food matters. You also need to take note of the service, the ambiance of the restaurant and decide on the value-for-money offered.

You must also be able to describe food accurately and fairly, and make your descriptions interesting. The successful restaurant review gives the reader a flavour of the meal, an educated opinion of the chef's abilities and enlarges his experience of food, all without being pretentious, negative or pompous.

6

SELLING ARTICLES AND BOOKS

You've got lots of ideas and you're convinced you can do better than many of the articles and books you see being published. How do you get editors to understand that a new talent is waiting to be discovered?

The approach for articles is slightly different from that for books and we will deal separately with each.

Selling articles

The range of publications offering opportunities to the free-lance writer is enormously wide. If you approach the market sensibly and produce work that is geared in the right way, there is no reason why you should not enjoy success and a rising acceptance rate.

We can divide the process of selling articles into the following stages:

- Researching the market
- Selling an idea
- Submitting an article
- Keeping track of submitted work
- A cuttings book

Researching the market

We have already talked about checking through newsagents' stands and reference books, recommending that recent copies of promising publications should be bought for closer study.

The cost of buying newspapers and, particularly, magazines these days can add up quite alarmingly; more so if you have to pay for them to be sent to you from circulation departments. If you then find out that you have misjudged, and the publications aren't offering a possible market for you, that is money wasted.

A solution to this problem is to ring up before buying. Ask to speak to the editor, explain that you are interested in writing for the publication and enquire whether freelance work is accepted. If the answer is 'no', you will have saved the purchase price. If the answer is positive you can then check exactly what sort of material is being looked for and can offer an idea for consideration. You will probably be asked to put it in writing before the editor will comment, but an initial contact will have been made. You should also ask what the rates of pay are. Some editors may say that fees are a matter for negotiation or that they depend on various factors, but others may well give you a figure. Keep notes of all such calls.

If you have followed the advice given so far, you should have identified various publications which accept freelance food or cookery articles. You will also have sorted out what their readership looks for, and should have a very clear idea of the market you could be writing for.

Now you need to consider the nature of your ideas and ensure that the basic theme of your article is suitable for your chosen publication.

For instance, an article on quick and easy but nutritious and tasty school lunch-boxes could appeal to a popular publication aimed at a family readership or young mums. One on the finer points of caviar and how it can be served would only be attractive to a publication with an up-market readership.

Some ideas, however, can be angled to suit a number of

different outlets. Take an article on casserole recipes, for instance. Concentrate on the cheaper cuts of meat and easy ways to achieve a dish full of flavour and it could be suitable for a general magazine or popular newspaper. Explore recipes from different countries, taking in cultural aspects, and it would be better suited to a broadsheet newspaper or a magazine catering for an up-market or specialist readership.

Consider, also, length. Some ideas need to be explored in depth while others are particularly suited to short and pithy pieces. It is no use sending a 2,500 word article to a journal that only ever publishes short pieces, nor trying to cram an idea that needs space into 500 words. Beware, though, of indulging yourself with words. The more succintly you can express your ideas, the more likely you are to achieve success. Remember that with recipe based articles, the recipes have to be the star feature; with non-recipe writing, it is the ideas that will command attention.

Selling an idea

Right! You have identified a possible publication together with an idea for an article. Now you have to sell it. There are two ways of going about this.

Professional writers will identify a likely market and then write to the editor, with a stamped addressed envelope, suggesting a particular topic. They will mention any expertise and experience they may have, ask how many words the editor might like to see and what the rates for contributors are. If the editor could be interested, he may ask to see the article before deciding if he can accept it.

If you follow this procedure and the answer is 'no', write to another editor. This way you maximise your efforts.

Unless your article requires a considerable investment of time in research and the development of your idea, the better course for a beginner is usually to send the finished work. This is because the editor has no way of knowing how good your work is or how reliable you are. With the article in front of him, he can make up his mind on the finished piece. Also, with recipe based work, ideas are often valuable and they can't be copyrighted. Send in an article – and your precious ideas are better protected.

The article will, of course, be written in such a way that it suits the chosen publication perfectly, be original, lively and the right length and include, if relevant, exciting recipes. How, then, can the editor refuse it? He may well not and you will have the excitement of receiving an acceptance letter. But he may have just accepted an equally suitable article submitted along the same lines and not need another. Or have just decided to make changes in the magazine that will mean your article no longer fits in with his editorial approach. Or perhaps your theme isn't one that attracts him. Is there some way you can make sure all your effort isn't wasted?

When submitting to a publication for the first time, you should include some details of your background which qualify you for writing the article. You can also say that you have other ideas and mention a couple. If you think the article you are submitting is capable of being turned into a short series, you should mention that as well. You are, in fact, offering not only the article being enclosed with the letter but also the opportunity for the editor to provide some encouragement for future articles, even if he has to turn down your initial one. Your letter could be along the following lines:

Dear Miss/Ms/Mrs Jones/Mr Smith,

I am enclosing for your consideration, at your standard rates, a 000 word article, DREAMY WAYS TO START DINNER, six ways to give a dinner party a good start.

I have been catering locally for some five years and have recently started writing articles on food and cooking. All the recipes are original; three have proved particularly popular with clients, the other three are new creations.

If it interests you, this article could be followed up with two more: DREAMY MAIN DISHES and DREAMY DESSERTS. Other ideas I think could be particularly suitable for your publication are: PORTABLE PICNICS, ideas for meals to take to outdoor events where space and facilities are limited; and INSTANT SUPPERS, family recipes that take less than twenty minutes to prepare. I would be delighted to send you the articles for consideration.

If the article is accepted, I would appreciate a copy of the magazine in which it appears. If not, please return it in the enclosed stamped addressed envelope.

Yours sincerely,

Encs: DREAMY WAYS TO START DINNER
SAE

Points to note are: the letter is addressed to the editor by name, which is easy to find out from a copy of the magazine or by ringing up the publication. You give the length of the article, state your qualifications for writing on cookery, assure the editor that the recipes are original, and give further ideas (without giving details of your precious, original recipes).

It does no harm to ask for a copy of the issue your article appears in and you may well receive one. Don't count on it though.

If the editor accepts your article, whether or not he says he is interested in any of the other ideas you mentioned, it is a signal that your work is suitable for the publication and you should follow up with further submissions. They may not always prove acceptable but if you can do it once, you can do it again. If you keep up a steady flow of good articles, one day you might even be asked to become a contributor on a regular basis. That is what happened to me and the *Daily Telegraph*; from writing occasional food pieces, I was asked to contribute first a monthly and then a weekly cookery article.

If the response to your letter and article is negative, don't despair. Find another market, rewrite the article if necessary to suit your new target, and repeat the exercise. There are writers who send off articles to more than one market at the same time, informing editors in a covering letter of their action. The advantage of this method is that your ideas are less likely to be pinched without the article being paid for; the disadvantage is that most editors dislike being hustled into decisions by the threat of someone else buying the article first, particularly from an unknown. They may even refuse to consider the article at all.

Keep covering letters as short as possible. Editors are busy people who want the salient facts, not a lot of chat. Don't say how marvellous the article is. It can and should speak for itself. If you feel you need to give more than the briefest of details about yourself, attach a separate Curriculum Vitae giving your background. Ideas for other articles could also be given on a separate sheet. Only give two ideas, or three at the most, in addition to the article you send. They will be enough for the editor to consider. Ideas are precious; you don't want to spread them around too freely.

With recipe based work, give the editor some idea of the visual quality of your recipes, or how they will look when prepared for photography. A stunning effect will almost certainly guarantee your article is seriously considered. Photographs could help here (*see* Chapter Nine).

Submitting an article

The presentation of your article, like your food, is important. A dish that doesn't look attractive has to work twice as hard at convincing the eater it's worth consuming. It's exactly the same with written work.

Articles should be typed. If you are using a typewriter, make sure your ribbon produces clear print. Correct errors neatly and keep them to a minimum. Type in double spacing with generous margins and don't justify the right hand margin, it should be left ragged. Each page after the title page should have the name of the article in the top left-hand corner, and you can also add your surname for complete security in case the pages become separated. Pages should also be numbered, usually in the top right-hand corner.

The title page doesn't need anything at the top. It should have the title of the article, in caps and usually underlined, centred about one third down the page. Give four line spaces, then centre your name, which can also be underlined. There should be another gap of four lines before starting the article.

The first line of the first paragraph of any article is started at the margin, while the first line of all succeeding paragraphs is indented.

For the layout of recipes, *see* Chapter Seven.

At the end of the article, type 'The End' or a little design like: – o0o – to show that it is finished. After that, add the approximate number of words on the left, rounded up to the nearest 50 words for articles up to 1,000 words long and up to the nearest 100 words for work over that length. Underneath, add: Copyright, followed by your name. Below that, in single spacing, write your name and address.

At least one cookery writer I know adds the copyright line at the bottom of every page of a recipe article. This is a sensible precaution as, particularly with recipes, pages of an article can get separated. It is wise to guard against unattributed use of your recipes.

Add a cover page. This should consist of the title of your article and your name as they appear on the first page, but centred in the middle of the page. Below that, on the bottom left-hand side, add the length as it appears on the last page, the copyright claim and your name and address. On the right-hand side of the page, level with the copyright line you can write: First British Serial Rights or FBSR Offered. That is almost certainly what will be bought even if you don't state it but there is no harm in making certain.

The point about FBSR is that those are the rights for first appearance in the magazine. Any other appearances have to be paid for. Also, and this is particularly important with recipe based work, you are retaining the right to sell the material for a second time. In other words, you are retaining the copyright of your work.

With straightforward articles, FBSR is not such an important consideration. Few editors want to print an article that has already appeared elsewhere (though these days newspapers are occasionally publishing articles that have previously appeared in specialist magazines) and if you want to use the material a second time, it is usually possible to rework the article in such a way that it becomes saleable again for the more valuable First Serial Rights. With recipes, the case is very different. A recipe is a complete creation that you may well feel shouldn't be altered in any way and that you could want to use in a book at some stage. You may even be able to use it in another article (though you will need to declare when submitting the article that one or more of the recipes have already been published and some considerable time will need to have elapsed). Always protect your copyright.

Staple the pages of your article together. This will help prevent them getting separated before acceptance.

If you are sending any illustrations, attach a separate caption page to your article, make sure each illustration can be matched to its caption, and add your name and address to the caption page and to the illustrations (*see* Chapter Nine). Do make sure illustrations are properly protected with a cardboard backing and never attach them to your work with a paper clip, as it can leave a mark on the print or transparency.

Make sure you keep a copy of your work. It is not unknown for articles to be lost, either in the post or from a busy editor's desk. If you keep your work on a word processor disk it is not essential to keep a hard copy but sensible to ensure you have a back-up copy.

Send a brief letter with the article (*see* page 67), and enclose an addressed envelope with enough postage stamps for the article's return if it should be deemed unsuitable. Try to send the article unfolded if possible, or, if you can't afford the large envelopes, fold it once. I save all large envelopes I receive and recycle them, on the basis that my article will probably be opened by a secretary before the editor sees it.

Having sent off your article, start on another so that if you do get rejected you already have something else in the pipeline.

Keeping track of submitted work

It's unusual but not unheard of for nothing to happen. If you don't receive any news or the article back after six weeks or so, send a follow-up letter to the editor, politely asking if a decision has been reached yet and repeating your request that the article be returned if it is unsuitable. It is worth adding that an SAE was included in the original mailing. If you still don't hear, ring up. It may be that the editor likes your article but hasn't an immediate use for it and is keeping it for possible inclusion at some unspecified future stage. This can be unsatisfactory but is better than an outright rejection.

Keep a book in which you record the title of the article, the publication/s to which it has been sent, the date of despatch, the date of acceptance or rejection, the date payment is received and the amount. It is then easy to check exactly what has happened to each of your articles and to follow your progress.

A cuttings book

Once an article of yours has appeared, make sure you get hold of a copy and paste it in a cuttings book. It's most satisfactory to see the cuttings gradually build up and once you have a good acceptance record behind you, copies of suitable cuttings can be sent with enquiry letters to new publications. This will give the editor a chance to judge your work and see if he thinks it could be suitable for his journal. Also, if your work is recipe based it is a good way of keeping track of which of your recipes have already been published.

Selling books

The process of selling a book is rather different. To start with, it is almost always a waste of time actually to write your book before trying to find a publisher. It sounds odd, but food and cookery books today have to be so tightly tailored to particular markets, that the chances are you would have to rewrite your book before it could be published!

The selling of a book can be divided into the following stages:

- Researching the market
- Producing a synopsis
- Sample chapter/recipes
- Approaching an agent/publisher/manufacturer

Researching the market

Researching the market, in this instance, means not only checking to see which publisher is a likely target for your book idea but also what chances it will have for success.

Your publisher will need to be convinced that there is a readership waiting for your work. So, first, try to find out if your idea, or one close to it, has been produced by anybody else. A bookshop with a large cookery section or a specialist outlet such as Books for Cooks will probably be able to help here. Check several sources.

Ideally, you should find that no one has written anything like your work. Or you may find something similar has appeared and be able to show why it doesn't provide competition. Perhaps the other book is badly flawed in some way, or published sufficiently long ago for a new approach to be valid.

You should also try to show not only that there is nothing similar to your work on the market, but that there is a need for it. It could be that nobody has thought it worthwhile to cover the subject and it is up to you to demonstrate that there are large numbers of readers out there just waiting for your book.

With my book *Just for Two*, I identified various groups who needed recipes designed for two people: newly marrieds, couples whose children have left home, two people sharing a flat, single people who prefer to entertain just one other person. They all add up to a sizeable section of the population. I was also able to show that there was very little catering for them and nothing as comprehensive as the book I was proposing.

At the same time as you are checking out possible competition for your idea, look and see which publishers are putting out the sort of book you think yours will be, and make a note of their names. Some publishers produce a wide range of food and cookery books, others specialise in particular areas. Just as it is no use giving meat to a vegetarian, so it is useless offering a small, gift type recipe book to a publisher who specialises in producing chef's books.

Producing a synopsis

In order to sell your book, you need to make a synopsis of its contents. It need not be long (standard advice is two to three pages), but more detailed ones can also be successful.

The aim of the synopsis is twofold: first, to interest the publisher in your idea and, second, to demonstrate that you are capable of producing the book as you suggest.

The synopsis should, therefore, be in several parts. First, a short introduction putting forward a brief outline of the book, why you want to write it and its probable length, either in terms of words or, if it's cookery, number of recipes. The introduction is the most important section of your proposal for, if the basic idea fails to interest the publisher, it is most unlikely that any of the rest of your submission will be read.

The next bit should contain your market research; why your book is needed and why it will be unique. Identify any possible competition and then explain why it won't affect the prospects for your book.

After that, give a brief description of your qualifications for writing the book, including details of any published work.

Then, detail the chapters with a brief description of their contents. This could include a selection of recipe titles.

Finally, if your idea is for a food book, you should offer to produce a sample chapter. If it is for a cookery book, it is a better idea to include some sample recipes with your synopsis so that the publisher can judge your ability.

Your submission should look as professional as possible. As with articles, it should be typed in double spacing. If you are using a typewriter with a faint ribbon, invest in a new one, preferably one of the carbon types that produces very crisp printing. The typing should be perfect, any corrections unspottable. The finished product must be pristine.

Prepare a title and cover page just as suggested above for articles. The only differences should be that you won't include a word count and the copyright line won't include a reference to FBSR.

Don't staple the pages together. If you like, you can place them in a folder or some binder which is easily taken apart. Editors find it much easier to assess work if they can handle the pages separately.

Invest in a sturdy A4 envelope that will take the pages without being folded, for editors prefer to consider manuscripts that lie flat on the desk.

Sample chapter/recipes

As suggested above, if you are proposing a food rather than a cookery book, you can indicate that you would be willing to produce a sample chapter, if the publisher is interested, rather than sending one with your synopsis.

If your offer is taken up, the publisher may suggest a particular chapter or give you the choice. Whichever chapter you submit, it must be the best work of which you are capable, for it will be your flagship. Presentation of it will be exactly the same as for your synopsis, with cover page, title page, copyright line and your name and address, plus a word count.

If you are proposing a cookery book, unless your work is well known or you can include some suitable cuttings of published articles, it is almost essential to provide sample recipes with your synopsis. These will give the publisher a feel for your approach to cooking and your ability to create attractive, original and workable recipes.

You can produce either a sample chapter or a selection of recipes from a number of chapters.

Together with the basic idea, it is your recipes that will sell your book. They should be original (*see* Chapter Eight), appealing and well presented (*see* Chapter Seven). Above all, they should capture the flavour of the proposed book. Presentation is the same as for a sample chapter and a synopsis (*see* above).

Approaching an agent/publisher/manufacturer

Having got your synopsis together, the next stage is to decide where to send it.

You can go direct to a publisher, or you can try to find an agent to represent you.

An agent will take a percentage of any contract he arranges for you (usually between 10 per cent and 15 per cent). You may think this quite a lot of money but there are many advantages to having an agent. First of all, there are publishers who won't accept unsolicited manuscripts (and that includes a synopsis) for consideration unless it's presented by an agent. An agent will also scrutinise any contract offered and may be able to negotiate better terms for you than you could yourself.

Publishers will claim, particularly with a first book, that they issue standard contracts with standard advances. However, there are some unscrupulous publishers around and I have heard the odd horrific story of unwary beginners who were so keen to get their precious book in print that they have signed contracts which barely paid them enough to cover their expenses. An agent will protect you from any such experience, and they are almost always trustworthy. There is an Association of Authors' Agents and its members operate by a code of conduct, expelling members who, for instance, transgress by charging extortionate commission rates.

A good agent will justify his existence by selling further rights to your books. It is just possible to sell a book to a British publisher yourself but it is very difficult to market the foreign and other rights.

Finally, being represented by a reputable agent is probably your best protection against your valuable ideas being pinched and given to some other writer to develop. As I've said already, ideas are not copyright, and it is extremely difficult to prevent others making use of them; but few publishers will want to risk a rift with a major agent by an act of piracy.

Finding a good agent, though, is almost as difficult as finding a publisher. The two writers' handbooks already mentioned (*see* Appendix) give lists of agents. Most of these give a brief description of the sort of works they are prepared to handle.

Approach possible agents with a preliminary letter to make sure they would be willing to consider your synopsis before you send it to them.

Personal recommendation is probably the best way to find an agent, so try to find an author friend who is satisfied with his representation and ask if his agent would be prepared to consider taking you and your book on as well.

But if you prefer to approach a publisher directly, or you can't find an agent willing to take you on, you should take the list that you have prepared of publishers producing books similar to yours and check whether they consider unsolicited manuscripts. Usually, if they won't, they state this underneath their entry in the writers' year books. However, before sending off your outline, ring them up to make sure and also find out the name of the cookery editor. Then you can address a personal letter to send with your synopsis.

Introductory letters should be brief, to the point and always sent to the right person by name. Include an SAE for return of the synopsis if it proves unacceptable.

Manufacturers often sponsor books that promote their product, be it an ingredient or a piece of equipment (*see* Chapter Four). Very often they will approach a particular writer for a book they have in mind but sometimes an outline for an unsolicited idea attracts them. The recent economic climate has drastically reduced the number of these books being produced but things may improve.

If you have an idea which you think could interest a particular manufacturer, the procedure is exactly the same as given above, including ringing up the manufacturer to find exactly to whom to send your synopsis.

Once you have submitted your synopsis, you will have to wait. Sometimes you will receive a response within two to three weeks. But publishers often need longer to consider an idea. If you haven't heard anything after six weeks, send a polite letter enquiring what the situation is. If you still hear nothing, don't be afraid to ring up after eight weeks to ask, again politely, what is happening to your idea.

If your idea is particularly topical, you can ask for a response within a certain time, say four weeks. Or you can send it, explaining what you are doing, to a number of publishers at the same time. This procedure can also go some way to preventing your idea being pinched by an unscrupulous editor, since a large number of people will know who has submitted it.

7

RECIPE WRITING AND ORGANISATION
OR
FIRST WRITE YOUR RECIPE THEN ORGANISE
YOUR WORK

No one can teach you how to create recipes. Putting ingredients together, devising attractive dishes with a difference, adapting techniques – all this has to be an individual process. Many cooks do it almost without thinking, while others spend hours refining recipes before they are happy with their dish.

Cooks also vary in the way they create their recipes. Some of us, myself included, create dishes in our heads, tasting the ingredients in our imagination, selecting cooking techniques. Then we write down a draft recipe before cooking it. More tasting then to assess the exact flavour, changing this and adapting that until the result satisfies. Others start with a collection of ingredients and an idea and put everything together as they cook, making notes on quantities and method, then writing up the recipe afterwards.

It doesn't matter how you create your dish. It is, though, important that the finished recipe is presented in a way that makes it easy for the reader to follow. Over the years certain recipe writing conventions, such as how ingredients are listed, have become accepted.

This chapter is all about how to write recipes and then incorporate them into a book.

The technique of writing a recipe

Up until halfway through the last century, the only way to find out what ingredients were needed for a recipe was to read through it. Then Eliza Acton produced a book with recipes that ended by repeating the ingredients in a list. It was a logical step and the mystery is why it took so long to happen.

Almost immediately, the practice was taken up and improved by setting the list of ingredients before the recipe. More recently, other developments have followed and most cookery writers now accept that there are conventions to recipe writing that need to be observed.

Writing a recipe for publication is, in fact, a more complicated process than initially appears. We can consider the main points under the following headings:

- Title
- Servings
- Order of ingredients
- Ingredient quantities
- State of ingredients
- Method
- Watchpoints and other additions

Title

The title of your recipe can be anything you like, its purpose being to identify the dish. It can be called after someone, like the Tarte Tatin, the classic French upside-down apple tart named after the sisters who created it in the last century. French is the language of haute cuisine but these days giving dishes French titles, unless they actually are French, is considered somewhat pretentious. Straightforward descriptions, that give you an indication of what sort of dish the recipe is, are the most popular today.

Servings

Readers need to know exactly how many people your recipe is supposed to serve. This can either be stated under the title or, if all the recipes are intended to serve the same number, at the beginning of the book or recipes.

Working out how many a recipe will serve can sometimes cause problems. If you are used to feeding very hungry teenagers, your recipe portions will be much larger than someone feeding, say, the elderly. Try to assess the amount your readers are likely to consider a reasonable portion, as it may differ from your usual amount.

Order of ingredients

Ingredients should be listed in the order that they will be used, not in their order of importance. Thus, if you are writing a recipe for a dish in which meat is marinaded before being cooked, you will put first the ingredients for the marinade, in the order in which you feel they should be added to the bowl, then the meat. Then you list the ingredients needed for the actual cooking, again in the order in which they are used.

Ingredient quantities

Now that the U.K. has gone metric, quantities are usually given in both metric and imperial measurements.

How do you convert quantities? The way I work is to take the main ingredient and find the nearest satisfactory metric equivalent. With imperial measurements, for instance, a cake recipe may call for 4oz flour, butter and sugar. The metric equivalent for 4 oz is 112 g, not a very satisfactory amount. So I use 100 g and adjust the other ingredients to match.

However, 8oz of flour is better treated as 225 g, which is almost exactly what it weighs, rather than 200 g. As long as you keep the ratio between the ingredients correct, you don't need exact equivalents. This is why recipes using both metric and imperial quantities should contain a warning to the cook not to mix the scales. For a casserole it mightn't matter but for baking the result could be disastrous. If you are converting from metric to imperial, you follow the same principle but the other way around.

A further difficulty enters if you are writing for America or the Antipodes, since they measure everything in volume. It all stems, I am sure, from pioneering days when scales were in short supply but all cooks had a cup around and used that as their measuring tool. At some stage, the amount a cup held was standardised at half a pint. Enter another complication. The U.K. pint contains 20 fl oz; the U.S. pint 16 fl oz. So a cup measurement for American recipes holds 8 fl oz.

The process of converting recipes into volume measurements can be a tedious business since the volume of 200 g sliced mushrooms, for example, will be different from 200 g of almost anything else. Eventually, though, you get into the swing of it and build up a table of equivalent measurements.

State of ingredients

Ingredients should be expressed in such a way that the cook knows exactly how they should be prepared. This is a comparatively modern development. Recipes used to state: 8 oz mushrooms; then, under 'method', the cook would be told to slice them. However, preparation is much simpler if all the details don't have to be filleted out of the recipe before cooking starts.

If something needs slicing, chopping, blanching, or has to undergo any other procedure before it is used in the recipe, state this in the ingredient section.

There's another little refinement to ingredient listing that is important. Putting the preparation instructions after the ingredient means that your cook starts with the weight of the ingredient as purchased, then proceeds as instructed. This can often affect the finished weight of the ingredient. For instance, filleting and skinning a fish produces flesh that weighs much less than the whole fish. If your list of ingredients states: 500 g salmon, filleted and skinned, your reader will go out and buy a whole piece of salmon weighing 500 g; then bone and skin it. If you mean the cook to start with salmon flesh weighing 500 g, you should state 500 g filleted and skinned salmon. To be really helpful, and for complete clarity, you could also state how much unprepared salmon will probably be needed to end up with the right weight. This point needs particular attention if you are working in volume measurements; 1 cup of mushrooms, sliced, is a very different quantity from 1 cup of sliced mushrooms.

Try to avoid imprecise instructions. Dice come in a variety of sizes; do you want the cook to use large or small dice? Chopping a vegetable can result in quite large, medium or very small pieces, which do you mean? Exactly how thick or thin should the pastry be rolled out?

It's better not to use abbreviations for spoon sizes. They are easily misprinted or misread and the result can be disastrous, especially if more than one is involved.

Some recipe books have the ingredients centred on the page, while others line up on either the left or right hand margins. It doesn't matter which method you use for your presentation but make sure you remain consistent throughout your typescript.

Here is a very simple recipe that uses the accepted conventions:

Spicy Celery, Peppers and Tofu Stir-Fry

(Serves 2 people)

1 tablespoon light vegetable oil
1 clove garlic, peeled and finely chopped

Walnut sized piece green root ginger, peeled and finely
  chopped
3 stalks celery, trimmed
½ medium sized red pepper,
  trimmed   } All cut into thin strips
½ medium sized green pepper,
  trimmed
Salt and freshly ground black pepper
4–6 spring onions, dark green leaves and root ends
  trimmed off, onions split into strips same length as
  peppers and celery
2 teaspoons light soy sauce
1 tablespoon rice wine or   } All mixed together
  dry sherry
½ teaspoon chilli sauce
100g/4oz/¾ cup tofu cut into large dice before measuring

Garnish: a few toasted almonds

Method

Now you have to tell the cook how to produce the finished
dish and your instructions should be clear, concise and avoid
ambiguity. You need to give the inexperienced reader enough
information to ensure he produces a successful dish, without
boring the accomplished cook. Much, of course, will depend
on the amount of space you have, and how many words you
can afford to use. Some recipes break down 'method' into
numbered stages, which can be very helpful but takes up
more space.

The instructions for the above recipe run like this:

Method: Heat oil in a wok or large frying pan, add garlic
and ginger, celery and peppers, season and stir-fry for 1
minute. Add spring onions and stir-fry another minute, by

which time the vegetables should be tender but still slightly crisp. Add the spicy mixture and toss the vegetables, making sure they are well coated. Finally, add the tofu and stir gently for a brief period to mix and heat through. Check seasoning then serve immediately garnished with the toasted almonds.

Are you wondering why, having given the cook an exact amount of time to stir-fry the vegetables, I bother to say that after cooking, 'the vegetables should be tender but still crisp'? If the cook has cut the vegetables thicker than I intend, or not turned up the heat so high, they will take longer to cook. I could have written 'cook until tender but still crisp' but then some cooks wouldn't realise how short a time this takes. So I give what I judge to be the right amount of cooking time but also tell the cook exactly what state the vegetables should reach.

It is very easy to be ambiguous when describing method. 'Remove skin from cooked fish, flake and add to mashed potato', for instance. Is the cook supposed to flake the skin and bone or the flesh of the cooked fish? Which is supposed to be added to the mashed potato? You may not be in doubt but other readers might, especially with less obvious examples.

There are other points to consider. Should you state oven temperatures before the method? Breaking them out can be very helpful as ovens often need switching on before preparations start and it saves the cook having to skim through the recipe to find out what the temperature should be. But it can depend on the amount of space you have available.

While we are talking about ovens, remember that temperatures should be given in centigrade, fahrenheit and their gas equivalent. If you are familiar with the Aga and similar stoves, it can help to give some guidance on their use as well, as lots of people now cook with them.

You might also want to add microwave instructions if the recipe is suitable for cooking in that way.

If the recipe needs to be started well before the main

preparation, I like to note that above the list of ingredients. There is nothing more infuriating than deciding to cook an attractive-looking dish, making sure all the ingredients are to hand, then reading through the method and discovering that something needs marinading for twenty-four hours.

What about the equipment needed? Baking recipes should always specify the size of tin required and there are many other times when it is helpful to the cook to state what size of dish or bowl it is best to use.

Finally, does your method include all your ingredients? We have all met recipes where we were left at the end wondering what to do with a stray ingredient we prepared but were never told what to do with. It's very easy to omit an item, particularly when many get added to a dish at the same time. The best way to pick this up is to re-test the finished recipe (*see* Importance of accuracy, below).

Watchpoints and other additions

Explaining points of technique in a recipe can overload descriptions of method and irritate experienced cooks. A good way of getting round this is to add a 'Watchpoint' section at the end of a recipe if you feel beginners might need some help. For instance, with a meringue recipe you could add something like this:

> WATCHPOINT: Make sure you don't leave beaten egg white standing before adding the sugar; as soon as you stop beating, the foam will start breaking down. Watch also that you don't overbeat the whites, as that, too, will cause them to break down. Stop at the very glossy stage, before the foam becomes grainy.

Cook's Tips, Accompaniments and Variations are all useful additions to recipes.

For instance, to the above recipe could be added:

COOK'S TIP: An excellent chilli sauce can be made from marinading sherry with chilli peppers. Stuff a small bottle with the tiny chilli peppers sold by ethnic grocers, having first stabbed them all over with a pin (make sure you wash your hands carefully afterwards or you may irritate your eyes or mouth), pour over medium sherry, replace lid and leave for several weeks. Chilli oil can be made the same way and its bite is useful for many dishes.

ACCOMPANIMENTS: Rice and a salad would turn this dish into a substantial meal.

VARIATIONS: Greek feta cheese could be substituted for the tofu. Non-vegetarians could cook this recipe replacing the tofu with the same amount of uncooked chicken breast or fillet of pork cut into shreds. Stir-fry the meat before the vegetables, remove from wok and keep warm, wipe out wok with kitchen paper and heat another tablespoon of oil before proceeding as above, adding the meat instead of the tofu at the end.

Other information that could be added by way of symbols:

- Whether the dish will freeze
- An indication of how long the dish takes to prepare
- How expensive the dish is
- The level of technical difficulty involved

Importance of accuracy

Cookery writers always have to remember that readers will invest time and money in preparing their recipes. They do not want to be disappointed in the finished dish.

Never, ever, publish a recipe that hasn't been tested. No matter how convinced you are that the recipe works, cook it for yourself, or have it cooked by somebody else.

Mistakes are most usually made when a recipe is adapted from one already familiar. You know the original recipe works, you assume the new version will. But substituting one ingredient for another can sometimes lead to an unfortunate change in consistency. You may make a mistake in a quantity. If you are increasing or reducing amounts, you may over- or under-estimate the new cooking time or perhaps the new mixture won't fit the dish or tin specified. Always re-test.

Make sure your equipment is accurate. Do your scales weigh properly? Battery and pressure-operated scales are not always reliable, so check with a packet of butter that your scale registers what the packet states. If it's more than a fraction over or under, get the scales professionally checked. Balance scales should be accurate if the balance is perfect and the weights are kept clean.

What about your oven? Thermostats can be notoriously unreliable. Buy an oven thermometer and check the temperature in the middle of the oven. If you are uneasy about your oven's performance, arrange for it to be tested. A cake in your oven set at 190°C, 375°, Gas No 5, may bake perfectly but in a properly adjusted oven it might burn.

If you don't have them already, buy a set of measuring spoons. The ordinary table or teaspoon that you normally use may be different from that used by a reader. A proper measuring spoon, levelled off, conforms to a standard quantity.

When you are typing out your recipes, do check your copy carefully for printing errors are all too easy. A line can get missed from the list of ingredients, a quantity be misread, a repeated phrase in the method section can mean a typist's eye misses a whole part. Your checking of the final copy can't be too careful. Word processors have been of incalculable benefit to cookery writers: we can draft out a recipe, and then test cook it. At this point any errors invariably come to light. But the whole recipe doesn't need to be retyped, only the errors corrected on the disk before the recipe is reprinted.

All this effort is worthwhile when someone tells you how much they like your recipes 'because they always work'.

Now you know what to attend to when writing the recipes, what about the rest of the book?

Style

We all know what style is – the quality that makes an author's writing individual. Good style is attractive to read, while bad style comes between the reader and the message the writer is trying to convey.

That's easy enough to say, but how does someone not particularly talented with words acquire a good style? It can help to read writers whom you admire – but unless you allow your own personality to come through, your writing will never be as vivid as that of your role model and may well fail to make any impact at all.

Practice is the best method. The more you write, and try to get your information over simply, without fuss and frills, the easier you will find it and the more your writing will acquire a style of its own. Aim for short sentences and know exactly what you are trying to say. It can help to pretend your reader is in the room with you and you are talking to him. Read your work out loud. That always shows up awkward sentences.

The most effective cookery writers are those who convey exactly what they feel about food, their own thoughts and experiences. If you pick up one of John Tovey's books after seeing him on television or hearing him on the radio, you realise at once that he writes just as he speaks. Immediately you are in touch with his personality.

Introductions versus recipes

How far, in fact, should a cookery writer worry about literary style?

A quick browse amongst cookery books and articles will show that there is a wide diversity of approach. Some writers seem to enjoy wielding the pen as much as their cook's knife, while others keep the 'chat' to a minimum and get on with the recipes.

Each cookery book has to find its own balance between the explanatory introductions and the recipes themselves. The best guide must be your own feelings. Are you happy describing the very special qualities of a particular recipe? Does a dish need a preliminary explanation? Are there interesting things to say about where the recipe comes from, and how it was created? All these add to the reader's interest and expand his knowledge but it is perfectly possible to present recipes successfully without much introduction if that is what you feel happy with.

Do remember, though, that presenting recipes is just like food. The plainer a dish is, the better it has to be.

Whether or not you write introductions to your individual recipes, you will almost certainly need to write some sort of introduction to your book.

If your book is on a foreign cuisine, it will need to be placed in context. Historic, religious and social influences, regional variations, ingredients and cooking methods could all be gone into, in order to give the reader a background to place the recipes against.

If you are producing a definitive book on a particular technique, such as cakes or ice creams, you could go into method, equipment, history, ethnic variations and other aspects of your subject.

You certainly will need to present your theme and perhaps give some general notes on quantities, etc., but this need not take much space. A few paragraphs and you could plunge into the actual recipes themselves. Chapter Four looked more closely at the various ways in which a cookery book can be written.

Organising a cookery book

Your cookery book will need a coherent structure. Most follow one of the following formulae:

- The three-course meal
- Menus
- Generic
- Seasonal
- Techniques
- Alphabetical
- Idiosyncratic

The three-course meal

Now that entertaining is no longer so formal, this structure is a little old fashioned but, until recently, many cookery books used it. You begin with starters, sometimes subdividing them into soups, fish, salads, etc. Then you go on to main dishes; more subdivisions might be fish, game, chicken, beef, pork, etc. Finally, you end with desserts and sometimes an additional section on baking or preserves or anything else that doesn't fit your structure but which you want to include. The structure is still relevant for a book aimed at the market where dinner parties provide one of the main reasons for buying a cookery book.

A variation on this system is one that sorts recipes into sections for different types of meals: Breakfast, Lunch, Teatime, Picnics, etc.

Menus

This is the kind of book that devises a complete meal for all sorts of different occasions. As well as the recipes, it often offers shopping and organisational plans for each menu, usually concentrating on preparation beforehand and avoiding recipes that require last minute attention. It is very attractive to the person who entertains frequently and can cover a wide range of both events and recipes. The presentation is often very imaginative.

Generic

This is perhaps one of the most flexible of all systems. You group recipes according to their main ingredient or the type of dish. Thus you can have sections on: Cheese, Eggs, Fish,

Soups, Game, Poultry, Pasta, Grains, Seeds & Nuts, Vegetables, Fruits, Baking, Preserves, Bread, etc.

The advantage of this system is that it can be used to suit any type of cooking and can include a wide range of dishes. This doesn't mean, though, that it should be used as a catch-all for a pot-pourri of recipes that have nothing in common. As we discussed in Chapter Four, every cookery book must have a definite theme into which all its recipes fit.

This format can be applied to almost any kind of cook book, even those devoted to one type of food. Barbara Maher's classic *Cakes* (Penguin), divides her recipes into types of baking: Sponges and Biscuits, Choux Pastry, Meringues, Yeast Baking, etc.

Seasonal

This attractive format suits the cook who likes to work with seasonal produce. Basically, you divide your recipes between Spring, Summer, Autumn and Winter, or by month.

One of the best known books of this type is Margaret Costa's enormously successful *Four Seasons Cookery Book* (Sphere). She breaks each season down into sections that are different for each time of the year. Under Spring you find Pancakes, Easter Teas, Fish Soups, Scallops, etc.; Summer includes Cold Soups, Summer Starters, Crab, Cooking with Cream; Autumn has recipes for Mushrooms, Pizza and Savoury Pies; Winter includes sections on Comforting Breakfasts, Proper Puddings, Spices and so on. The recipes use not only ingredients but also techniques that are particularly appropriate to the season.

Techniques

This type of book organises recipes into sections covering techniques: Grilling, Braising, Poaching, Roasting, and so on. It is particularly suited to the writer who wants readers to understand how all cooking relies on the same basic rules. It can also be used to encourage readers to embark on their own recipe creation.

Alphabetical
Self-explanatory really. This format works very well for all sorts of encyclopaedic approaches, such as *Jane Grigson's Fruit Book* and *Vegetable Book* (Michael Joseph), where recipes are arranged under alphabetically ordered fruits and vegetables.

Idiosyncratic
Maybe you don't like any of the above formats and have a completely different idea of your own. Don't worry: as long as the reader can find his way round your book, you can organise your recipes exactly how you like. In *Just for Two*, I used a mixture: techniques (stir-fry, pancakes), generic, (fish, chicken, salads, sauces, etc) and the three-course meal (for a section on special meals for two). A geographical organisation could work for a book of regional dishes and there will be others that could interest you.

A really clever idea could sell a book on its own. Arabella Boxer's *First Slice Your Cookbook* (Nelson), had the pages cut into three. Starters were printed at the top, main courses in the middle and desserts at the bottom. The hostess could select her menu and then arrange the page parts so that all the recipes were open together for easy reference. It was a brilliant concept and the book is now a collector's item.

Other matters you might want to consider are whether or not you need a glossary and what to do about an index.

Glossaries

Do you need to describe exactly what you mean by 'sauté' when you use it in a recipe? Or what an unfamiliar ingredient is? Or a piece of equipment? This is where a glossary can come in useful. At either the front or the back of the book you can explain, in alphabetical order, all about techniques, unfamiliar ingredients, equipment and any other matters you think your reader would like to know about. Basic recipes can also be arranged in a separate section at the back of a book, which helps save repetition.

Indexes

All cookery books need an index. Your publisher may arrange for a professional to provide one. This is much the best system, as indexing is a skilled profession. However, you may have to produce it yourself. This calls for a painstaking reading of the text, noting every use of a particular ingredient, such as beef or red pepper, noting recipe titles, personal names and any other subjects you think the reader might want to look up, and arranging them in alphabetical order with all the page numbers. It's easiest done at page proof stage (*see* Chapter Ten) but can also be done in typescript, using the manuscript page numbers, which are amended later to the actual page numbers.

8

RECIPE COPYRIGHT AND CONTRACTS

Where do you get your recipes from? Do you have a file full of clippings from newspapers and magazines, recipes copied out from books and given by friends?

Or do you start with the ingredients, a basic knowledge of technique and create your own from scratch?

If that is the case, where do you get your ideas? Just from the ingredients themselves or are there other influences? Food you have eaten in restaurants here and abroad, perhaps? Dishes that had been given to you by friends? Cookery books and magazines that you read?

We are all influenced by everything around us. Somehow ideas become popular. In the early eighties the Scandinavian marinaded salmon delicacy, Gravad Lax, was everywhere. Chefs discovered it, writers included it in articles and in books, and you could hardly move in foodie circles without meeting it. A recent craze has been for roasted vegetables (traditionally popular in various Mediterranean countries).

These are both examples of what might be called 'ethnic dishes'. I have my own recipes for both. Or *are* they mine?

My mother is Swedish and I have known Gravad Lax since childhood; it is one of her specialities. She taught me how to make it and I then slightly adapted her recipe to my own taste.

When I used the Gravad Lax recipe in *A Little Scandinavian Cookbook* (Appletree Press), I wrote the following introduction:

The Norwegians and Swedes originally buried salmon as a means of preservation, using pine twigs or Scandinavia's favourite herb, dill, for flavouring. This recipe can also be used for trout or mackerel. A trout or mackerel will be ready in 24 hours, salmon will take 36-48 hours. Choose the middle cut of salmon or whole fat fish of the smaller varieties. Most Scandinavians use rather more salt than sugar but I prefer the slightly sweeter result given by equal quantities.

This introduction acknowledges the source of my recipe, in this case a popular tradition. I could have included a reference to my mother but I didn't have much space and I wanted to refer to her later in the book. The introduction also shows how my recipe varies slightly from what might be called standard ones.

I was introduced to roasted vegetables by Alicia Rios, a wonderful Spanish cookery writer. Shortly after learning about them from her, I found a couple of rather different recipes by other people. Experimenting with them all, I evolved my own way of preparing and serving them, which is different yet again. I haven't yet published my recipe but when I do I shall, again, give the background.

Every cookery writer should acknowledge their sources, and nobody should copy someone else's recipe without giving the original writer credit.

Copyright and plagiarism

When you write an article or a book, your copyright rests in the arrangement of words you have created rather than the ideas that have led to those words. If anyone publishes those words without your permission, they are committing plagiarism. Not so if they take the idea and incorporate it in a new work.

Copyright in cooking is a very grey area. If you take the basic idea of a recipe already published in a book, magazine or newspaper, change it very slightly, alter the wording, and print it under your name, it is unlikely that you will be sued for plagiarism, though wronged authors are beginning to try and the situation is changing. But you and everyone else familiar with the original recipe will know that you haven't actually created the dish.

Published recipes used to be considered fair game for anyone to play around with and claim they were theirs. Nearly every cookery writer, including me, has probably been guilty at some time of 'borrowing' a recipe, tinkering with it slightly and then considering it theirs.

Does this matter? Well, if the recipe you took was an original creation, that practice could be thought of as theft even if you have managed to avoid criminal liability. Also, most book contracts will require you to produce original recipes.

How do you decide if the recipe you have spent considerable time refining and working on is truly yours or if you should acknowledge someone else's input?

One yardstick is originality. Everybody involved with food spends a great deal of time working to create dishes that not only taste delicious but are different. It is sometimes said that everything in cookery has been done before but it *is* possible to come up with new twists and sometimes a truly original dish. One reason cookery writers are so keen to eat at top restaurants is because so often new ideas come from leading chefs.

Once they have found a new dish, writers naturally want to recreate it and tell other people about it. A cookery writer, recreating a top chef's recipe for the pages of a popular publication, or even a book, may change the list of ingredients slightly and adapt the method to cater for home cooks who have neither a chef's experience nor the facilities of a restaurant kitchen. So, the published recipe will probably not be the same as the one belonging to its originator. But the dish is still recognisable and at the very least the writer should acknowledge that the recipe is based on one created by so and so.

The same procedure should be followed with recipes from other sources that obviously have something different about them, even if you have changed them a little to suit your own purposes. You may, for instance, want to simplify the method or feel that you need to substitute a difficult-to-find ingredient for one more easily available; or you may just prefer a slightly different approach. You can't honestly say, though, that the recipe doesn't still basically belong to the person who originally wrote it. The correct procedure, again, is to say that this recipe is based on one created by such and such a writer or cook.

An argument is sometimes made that credit may be given to the wrong person. That the recipe writer you are acknowledging may have taken the idea, or even the whole recipe, from someone else. It is a hazard, but is that a reason to avoid giving an acknowledgement if you have no evidence it isn't justified?

We get into trickier waters with what might be called 'ethnic recipes', such as the two I referred to at the start of this chapter. These are recipes for traditional dishes common to regional areas. People have cooked them for many, many years and there are as many 'recipes' as there are cooks in that region. Into this same category can also come famous recipes that have been taken into the public domain, such as Tarte Tatin (the wonderful upside-down caramalised apple tart mentioned in the previous chapter), or Mère Poularde's incredibly light and fluffy omelette from Mont St. Michel. The original recipes for these dishes were probably never written down, have certainly been lost, and now we have subtle variations in ingredients, method and presentation – and endless arguments about the definitive version.

When I was developing recipes for both the little French and Scandinavian cookbooks that are published by Appletree Press, I collected any number of versions of each of the dishes. Some of these I had from French and Scandinavian friends and relations, others were found in books and cuttings. I prepared many of them and the receipes I eventually evolved captured, I hope, my personal impressions of the essence of each dish. At the end I felt that, though each dish was traditional, in most cases the recipe I was using could be called my own and the only acknowledgement needed was a general one such as that in the example above.

There are, though, occasions when you come across an original twist to a traditional recipe that captures your imagination. If you then publish your own recipe using that twist, you should acknowledge the source.

Finally, there are standard recipes from which it is impossible to deviate and whose origins, again, have been lost: Victoria Sponge, for instance. If you want to include a recipe for this classic cake, the only difference between your version, and that printed already in countless books and articles, will be small variations in the wording of the method. You can't get away from that and nobody expects you to.

There are, though, occasions when we think we are being original but are later accused of 'borrowing'. How can this happen?

Over the years we all read many different recipes. Without conscious thought, ideas lodge at the back of the mind which sometimes surface long after. They seem original to us, for we have genuinely forgotten reading the basic idea in some-one else's work.

Coincidence also plays a part. Ideas have their time and various influences can lead people to think along the same lines, so that two people may well conceive the same sort of recipe independently.

The Guild of Food Writers is currently working on a code of conduct that will give guidelines on acknowledging other people's creative work, which members will be expected to follow. By the time this book is in print, it should be available and may well clarify and further define what I have suggested above.

At one time editors disliked it if the writers whom they were paying for their expertise gave credit to other people. If an acknowledgement was put in the original copy, it was often removed before the article was printed (most authors have no control over what happens to their work after it reaches the editor's desk). Nowadays, it is increasingly recognised that credit has to be given where it is due and that, if all books and articles relied solely on truly original recipes, very little would get published.

In fact, it is not unusual now to see cookery writers including in their articles whole recipes taken from someone else's book, with proper acknowledgement. It is not lazy writing; the recipe may fit in with a particular theme, or the book may just have been published and the article writer wants his readers to know how good it is. If you want to include a recipe like this in either an article or a book, permission should be sought from the publishers of the original source for its use and full acknowledgement should be given (the recipe should also have been tested by the person including it in their work).

Professional cookery writers are now much more conscious of their responsibilities in this field and most try very hard to avoid passing off someone else's work as their own.

Protecting your own copyright

You will be as keen as anyone to protect your work when it starts to appear in print. As you can see from the above, that isn't always easy but there are certain safeguards you should take.

Copyright has to be stated. When submitting work, always write on the front page and at the end of the work: Copyright: followed by your name. You can also add the year. A capital 'C' with a circle round it symbolises the same thing.

I have already mentioned that it is a good idea, when submitting articles with recipes, to add this copyright line at the bottom of each page containing a recipe. This helps safeguard recipes being wrongly attributed if a page is separated from the main body of the article. The editor may not, in the end, use the article but the recipe could surface at a later date and be incorporated into another feature by mistake.

Contracts for books should have a 'Defence of Copyright' clause inserted in them. This will ensure that if some or all of the contents of your book are printed elsewhere without permission, the publisher will pursue damages and seek an acknowledgement.

Incredible as it may seem, there are instances of cookery writers finding large chunks and even whole books of theirs appearing in other countries under someone else's name.

If this happens, not only are the original writers suffering a loss of money, they are also being, in the words of one unlucky writer 'made invisible'. If this happens to you, make sure you pursue the publishers for restitution and proper acknowledgement.

There are a number of instances of writers pursuing publishers of articles or books plagiarising their works. They have insisted that proper acknowledgement of the copyright infringement should be made, and have also demanded damages – but asked for these to be sent to charities. To them, the loss of their copyright is much more important than loss of earnings.

Importance of scrutinising contracts

One of the advantages of having a good agent is that your contract will be properly scrutinised. Though most publishers will claim that their contracts are standard, an agent can often obtain a better deal for the client, particularly where subsidiary rights are concerned. And there are unscrupulous publishers around who will take advantage of the inexperienced writer who is so thrilled to have his work accepted, that he will sign anything.

If, however, you haven't got an agent and, miraculously, someone wants to publish your book, what should you do?

The following advice is not comprehensive but should alert you to some of the more common pitfalls:

As a start, you should check that any money you are being offered is an advance against royalties and not a one-off payment. Writers are always recommended never to sell their copyright for a lump sum. The publishers may make a fortune and you will have no come-back. Also check that the advance is non-returnable even if your sales do not come up to expectation and the book doesn't earn the advance.

Scrutinise the percentage royalty being offered and consult the Society of Authors if you feel that it is inadequate. 10 per cent of the book's sale price on hardbacks and 7½ per cent on paperbacks is the norm, though there is usually a caveat on copies sold at less than the usual wholesale price and, these days, more and more are suffering this fate as bookshops flex their buying muscle.

Check that you are not being expected to provide illustrations at your own cost. This can mean you end up paying for your book to be published. Is your royalty being shared with a photographer?

See what subsidiary rights are being bought and what percentage you are being offered for them. Subsidiary rights can include foreign rights (the sale of your book to be published in another country), paperback rights, large print rights, book club rights, serial rights (some magazines and newspapers can make substantial payments for the right to publish all or part of your book in their pages before or on publication), video and cassette rights, television and cinema rights. This list is by no means exhaustive but you can see that there are many different ways your book can earn money beyond the simple production of an initial hard or softback edition. Question your publisher on the number of copies being printed; check a 'moral rights' clause is being included, this protects your work from being adapted without your permission; ask for consultation on jacket design. Make sure that the clause concerned with final payment on publication includes a statement setting a time limit so that you get the money before the book appears if publication is delayed beyond a certain period.

Many reputable publishers have signed agreements with the Society of Authors and the Writers' Guild which bind them to a code of conduct designed to protect the interests of writers. Check and see if your publisher is one of these. It isn't a complete guarantee but should mean you are reasonably safe.

The Society of Authors will give advice on contracts, and writers' handbooks (see Appendix) usually have articles on what to look out for. It can also be helpful to try to get hold of a standard contract and compare it with the one you are being offered.

Always get everything in writing

Whether you are talking with publishers of books, magazines or newspapers, make sure everything that is agreed is confirmed in writing. This applies to fees, deadline dates, details of content of the work you are to submit, illustrations, when you will be paid and anything more you can think of. If necessary, write to them yourself, stating what has been agreed and asking for acknowledgement. It can save much heartache later on if you can refer to a letter rather than to a conveniently 'forgotten' telephone conversation.

9

ILLUSTRATIONS

Food is very visual. We eat with our eyes before we actually taste, whether it's a ripe peach or a beautifully presented dish. Over the last couple of decades more and more food and cookery books have been generously supplied with colour photographs. From miraculous dishes created by haute cuisine chefs and plated on stylish china to still-lifes of fruit and vegetables from Dutch masters, readers are tempted to relish pictures before words.

Not always, however; for some cookery books are still published with no illustrations at all. Is this how you see your book or do you want pictures? If so, what sort? And what about articles; how do they get illustrated?

This chapter is all about illustrations, whether or not they are necessary, what the choices are and how they can be obtained.

Before we consider the various needs of articles and books, let us look at the subject of what sort of illustrations can be considered. They can be divided into the following categories:

- Food photography
- Other photography
- Printed pictures including picture research
- Drawings and paintings
- Your own illustrations – if you are an artist
- Illustration as instruction
- Decoration rather than illustration

Food photography

While any reasonably intelligent person with a modern, automatic camera should be able to take general photographs worthy of publication, food photography is a highly specialised area.

Look at the photographs in any glossy magazine or recent cookery book, the majority of which will be in colour. Note how perfect the food looks. What seems an artlessly arranged plate of meat and vegetables will have had each item carefully placed for maximum effect. Large quantities of ingredients may have been rejected before the perfect samples shown in the final photograph were selected.

The food will have been prepared by a food stylist, someone with a particular talent for presentation. Often, several samples of the same dish will be cooked before the perfect photograph can be achieved.

Sometimes, though, particularly with regional and ethnic foods, a cookery writer has a specialised knowledge of how the dishes should look. In these cases it is often preferable for the author to insist he rather than a stylist prepares the food, so that it will look just as it should.

Preparing the food is only the start. It all has to be presented on suitable crockery with a background that fits in with the general appearance of the magazine or book in which the photographs will appear. Some photographs are shot on location: picnics, for instance, or meals served in grand surroundings or in a particular kitchen. Mostly, though, backgrounds are designed in the studio or the publication's kitchen.

Finally, all is ready for photography. This is, also, far from a simple matter, for not only has the shot to be perfectly composed, but the technical details will test the skills of any photographer. If you check picture credits, you will soon notice that there are a handful of food photographers who get used again and again, proving their mastery of this difficult field.

All this is not to say newcomers can't break into the field – just that it needs skill and dedication.

Other photography

If your writing is non-recipe based, photographs could offer attractive illustration possibilities. The main criteria are that the photographs should be relevant to the text, sharp and clear.

Equip yourself with a reasonable camera and study the basic requirements for taking properly focused, well-composed photographs. There are a number of excellent books available.

Take your camera with you everywhere so that no opportunity for interesting shots is lost. Food producers, markets, displays of food, equipment, kitchen interiors; take photographs of them all. You never know when they may be useful. Always note down all necessary details, including names and addresses of anyone prominently featured so that permission to use the shot can be obtained, or get a release signed on the spot. Before photographing on private property, ensure that there are no objections and, again, obtain a release for the use of any of your photographs.

Any shots not being used immediately should be filed, with the negatives in case you need prints. File, with your shots, details of when and where the photograph was taken, with full caption details, any releases obtained, the copyright position, etc.

Some publications require black and white photographs. Prints should be glossy and $10'' \times 8''$ is the preferred size. Others need colour and that means colour transparencies. 35 mm is generally acceptable. A black and white photograph can be made from a colour transparency but it is rarely as sharp as one originally taken in black and white and the process can be expensive.

All photographs should be captioned before being sent out for possible publication. Don't forget to include complete details of what is shown and a note of to whom the copyright belongs. It is wise to make sure the article or book for which the illustration is intended is also identified on the caption, and to submit a list of illustrations supplied.

Tom Jaine's *Cooking in the Country* (Chatto and Windus), provides an excellent example of the use of photographs, black and white in this instance. The book is a seasonal diary, centred on the famous Carved Angel restaurant in Dartmouth Tom Jaine created in partnership with its chef, Joyce Molyneux. The book concludes with a selection of recipes. The photographs, though, taken by James Ravilious, are not of food but illustrate various aspects of country life as it affects the production of food, adding an extra dimension to the text.

Printed pictures including picture research

Many articles and books make use of a wide variety of printed pictures obtained from many sources. Plates from old books and magazines, cartoons, picture postcards, menu cards, advertisements, and many more featuring food, equipent and related subjects can offer excellent illustrations.

Photographs and a variety of printed illustrations are available on loan from specialist libraries, who will charge for both the loan and future use. These costs can mount up alarmingly. Care must be taken to return the illustration in the same condition as it was loaned out.

Photographers own the copyright of their photographs, just as writers do their words. Credit must always be given where it's due and payment liabilities checked out before offering them for publication.

It is also possible to build up a collection of copyright-free illustrations. Old cookery books can offer a wide selection of charming engravings (*see* over), which will be out of copyright fifty years after their author's death. Keep your eyes out for old postcards and other food-related items in second-hand book shops, bric-a-brac stores and other places. Caroline Liddell and Robin Weir's book, *Ices The Definitive Guide* (Hodder & Stoughton), uses a mix of many different kinds of illustrations which relate in various ways to the ice and its

Spinning sugar from Mrs A. B. Marshall's *Larger Cookery Book of Extra Recipes*, 1891.

history: sketches of equipment, old photographs and post-cards, advertisements, engravings and plates from old books, photographs of equipment, cartoons and even postage stamps. Many of these are owned by the authors. The list at the front of the book which credits the remaining illustrations provides an interesting example of varied sources and reflects the book's exhaustive study of its subject.

Picture research is a subject and career in its own right and some publishers employ a researcher to find suitable illustrations for many different types of books and articles. Occasionally the cost is charged to the author. Contracts should always be checked for any mention of liability for providing illustrations.

Copyright-free sources, which are unlikely to charge for supplying photographs (either black and white or transparencies), include public relations offices. The world of food is full of them. Either working in independent companies or directly employed, PRs promote the interests of, amongst others, producers, manufacturers, associations and countries. Good ones are enormously helpful, not only with illustrations but also with information. If you are writing about olive oil, for instance, there is an Olive Oil Information Bureau which will be delighted to help and may well be able to offer useful photographs. Embassies can also prove helpful, particularly if you approach them in good time. Some, like Spain, have special departments devoted to the promotion of their food and wine. Most manufacturers are also interested in promoting their products and that includes the supply of photographs.

Drawings and paintings

Drawings and paintings can convey an excellent impression of every aspect of food. Pen and ink sketches, engravings, pencil or crayon drawings, watercolour washes and other techniques have all been utilised by food and cookery writers.

Black and white drawings are very popular, particularly with what might be called 'literate' cookery books, which extend the reader's knowledge of the background to each recipe, the ingredients and other aspects. They are considerably cheaper to reproduce than colour and, while they lack its impact, can be strong on atmosphere.

Cartoons can also be extremely effective, adding a light note that is very attractive even if the book itself isn't humorous.

Paintings can contribute immeasurably to the atmosphere of a food or cookery book. I have contributed three books to a charming series of 'Little' cookery books published by the Appletree Press of Belfast. Nearly every recipe in each book is illustrated by a painting. Sometimes the illustration is of the prepared recipe, sometimes the ingredients, and sometimes both.

Employing an artist in this way can immediately make a cookery book look attractive and provide the recipes with a visual personality. Most publishers are very careful to match the right artist to the right author.

Your own illustrations – if you are an artist

Paying someone for illustrations is usually expensive but perhaps you are something of an artist yourself? There are a number of food and cookery writers who have illustrated their own work, Elizabeth Luard and Leslie Forbes amongst them.

Clarity is the first requirement for both sketches and illustrations; the reader must be able to recognise exactly what is being shown. Atmosphere is the second requirement. For good examples of both see Leslie Forbes' *A Table in Tuscany* (Webb & Bower, Michael Joseph). The book is an exploration of food from the heart of Italy. The author has illustrated her food experiences on her travels through Tuscany and decorated each page with colourful mementos. Landscapes, plates of food, sometimes partially consumed, maps, ingredients, labels, portraits of personalities met on her journey; these are just some of her subjects. The illustrations pepper the text and come in all sizes: sometimes small, a leaf or a couple of mushrooms, sometimes large enough to take up half or all of the page. They enlarge on the recipes and descriptions, enabling the reader to enjoy the book on several different levels.

Another aspect of Leslie Forbes' book worth noting is that the text isn't typeset but written in a beautifully clear hand. This is an approach which isn't used very often but can, as in this case, be extremely successful. Handwritten texts are usually combined with sketches or drawings. In *A Table in Tuscany*, the text flows around the illustrations and combines with them to form a very satisfying design.

With handwritten texts, it is essential that the reader has no difficulty in making out the recipes. Something that looks beautiful but is time-consuming to make out will have difficulty in finding a market. Also make sure your careful calligraphy will find a publisher before embarking on the writing of an entire book.

Illustration as instruction

Some techniques are easier shown than described. The way to chop an onion, bone out a chicken or carve a leg of lamb can be demonstrated in a sketch much more quickly than explained in words.

When sketches are used, they should be drawn from life so that the reader is in no doubt about what is being demonstrated.

Some books are almost entirely composed of explanatory photographs. These are expensive to produce and usually aimed at a mass market so that the cover price can be kept to a reasonable level.

Decoration rather than illustration

Some books are not so much illustrated as decorated. Fancy borders, a few line drawings, flourishes around chapter headings; these can be used to break up the text rather than illustrate the recipes.

If you are considering self-publishing, *see* Chapter Eleven. For non-copyright decorative touches, the American Dover Publication books of copyright-free artwork are published in the U.K. by Constable & Co. Food and drink-based images are included. Their drawback is that the artwork can appear in other works as well as yours.

Illustrating articles

Articles that need illustrating often stand a better chance of being bought if they arrive complete on the editor's desk.

Exceptions are the recipe based articles published by top magazines which like to organise their own photography and often have their own kitchens. Their editors know which stylist can achieve the effect they want and how to match the work of photographers to particular writers.

However, such magazines like to be given some idea of the visual quality of the dishes in the article they are being offered. Either add a description of the presentation or include a photograph of the finished dish for the editor's reference.

For other, less well-equipped magazines, however, a writer with a real talent for food presentation who can team up with a photographer and offer top quality illustrations along with the recipe article, should have an increased chance of publication. The stress, though, has to be on 'top quality'.

Even if you can't find a suitable photographer with whom to ally yourself, you can offer your food presentation skills along with your article, if you feel sufficiently confident.

Food articles featuring subjects such as producers, regional angles, produce, etc., will almost certainly be more acceptable if accompanied by relevant photographs and these can often be supplied by the author (*see* Other photographs, above).

Some articles may need other sorts of illustrations. I've written a whole series of articles on historical aspects of food for *Country Life*. The first of these was on quinces and I found some charming illustrations in old horticultural volumes at the Royal Horticultural Society Library. All the details were given to *Country Life*, who then organised the photography. For later articles, they carried out the picture research themselves.

Books

When you are considering the design of your book, give serious thought to what sort of illustrations you would prefer.

Much will depend on the sort of book it is. Books on various aspects of the food world often don't need pictures. Cookery books, however, gain considerably from almost any sort of illustration.

Many readers, particularly of family and popular type recipe books, want a photograph of practically every recipe so that they have an idea of what the dish should look like when they have cooked it.

Other readers are happy not to have all the recipes illustrated but like to be tempted by a selection of glossy colour photographs.

If you want photographs, consider whether you have the skills to produce and style the food yourself. Some publishers will be happy to allow you to, while others will want a professional food stylist.

There are, though, books that sell very successfully without any photographs at all. Very often, they are by authors with a gift for painting pictures in words. They convey the essence of each dish in their text. Sometimes, these books are illustrated here and there with line drawings, occasionally including an explanatory sketch or two for certain techniques.

Have a very clear idea of exactly how you would like your book to be illustrated – including the cover – before approaching a publisher. It is wise, though, to prepare yourself to be flexible.

A publisher may well be interested in buying your book but not in illustrating it in the way you would prefer. Cost is usually the major factor. Photography is very expensive and anything that raises the price of a beginner's book is likely to run into publisher resistance.

Commissioning photographs or artwork is only part of the expense involved in illustrating a book. Even line drawings can increase a book's cover price beyond what a publisher may think the market will accept.

10

BEING PUBLISHED

The miracle has happened and your article or book has been accepted. You have delivered your agreed manuscript by the given deadline and it's proved acceptable. What happens next?

Editorial process

The editorial process involved in having a book published is very different from that of an article. Let us look at books first.

First of all, you will meet your editor. This is the person who will be responsible for seeing your book on to the bookshelves. Yours will not be the only book he or she will be responsible for and anything you can do to ensure it gets maximum care and attention will be to the benefit of both you and your book. Try, therefore, to establish a good relationship.

The editing process calls first for the text to be scrutinised. This stage may be carried out by a freelance copy editor working together with the publishing company editor. Changes could be suggested. You may be asked to shorten, or lengthen (though that is less likely) certain sections. A few additional recipes may be requested, perhaps to help the layout of the book. A fresh eye may spot ambiguities in the recipe text or points of technique that haven't been sufficiently well explained.

It is always difficult to accept critical comments on one's work, even if the comments are constructive, but this is an important stage in your book's publication and you need to be as co-operative as possible. This does not mean that you have to accept every suggestion made to you if you don't agree with all of them. Something that appears irrelevant to your editor may be important to you. Explain why you don't agree, and your point may be accepted or at least a compromise suggested. Always remember that it is *your* book that is being published.

There will probably be a discussion on the design and you should have as clear a picture as possible of how you would like your book to look. You may have to change this, if it doesn't agree with the policy of the publishing company that has bought your book, but it will help if you can contribute definite ideas.

Have a look at recently published cookery books in a good booksellers. Note the various design options: how the text can be laid out on the page, how lines can be used to separate explanatory or introductory text from recipes and/or ingredient lists from recipes, the use that can be made of symbols, how certain information can be highlighted. Think about the cover (*see* below).

With articles, the author is rarely involved in the editorial process. Sometimes, usually for recipe based articles for a magazine, you will be sent page proofs to correct. Newspapers, though, generally do this in-house. Editors occasionally reword bits and often cut them without referring back to the author; there is very little that can be done to control the final appearance of your work. Make sure you don't go over the number of words that has either been suggested by the editor or which you have worked out is usually acceptable. Even this isn't foolproof, particularly with newspapers where advertising always has first claim on space.

An important point to note when you have an article accepted, is that newspapers will expect to get an invoice before sending out payment. Once you know what you will be paid, type out a simple one on your headed paper and send it in, adding VAT if you are registered. Magazines may or may not pay without an invoice first, check to make sure.

Choice of book covers

A good cover can mean a bookseller takes an unknown author's work, even, perhaps, features it. A potential reader will initially pick up a book because its cover catches their eye. It therefore deserves the closest consideration.

When my book *Just for Two* was being designed, I went and chatted to my local bookseller, who was very helpful. He pointed out how important the spine was because when the book is placed next to others on the shelf, that is all the customer will see. Designs that wrap around spines and carry on over the back of the cover can be very effective and make yours the book that is picked out.

Initially, I'd thought of having a picture on the cover with two plates of food sitting on a table. Looking at other covers, however, I realised that the choice of plates, food styling and table would immediately place the book in a certain class and I didn't want that, as I thought it had the potential to attract a wide range of people. Eventually, I suggested that we feature different ingredients in pairs: two fish, two chops, two carrots, two leeks, two cherries and so on. The editor produced examples of work from several photographers and together we decided on one with a talent for atmospheric but anonymous backgrounds. The result was a cover with which both I and the editor were very happy. I was lucky, though, for some publishers design covers without any reference to the author.

Proof reading

After your manuscript has been designed and typeset, you will be sent a set of proofs to correct. It is a good idea to check when they are likely to arrive and to make sure you are not going to be away or hopelessly busy then. The amount of time you will be given will vary, but it is rarely very long, three or four weeks at the most, sometimes less, especially if there has been a delay anywhere along the line.

Proof reading is always a somewhat tedious task and proof reading recipes is worse than most other texts, since it is imperative that the lists of ingredients are scrupulously checked. Check not just that the amounts are right, but that all the ingredients have been included, for it is very easy for type setters to miss a line.

Printer's proofs should be corrected according to an accepted set of symbols. *Writers' & Artists' Yearbook* (*see* Appendix), includes an easy-to-follow guide to correcting proofs. Use a red pen for correcting printing errors and a blue or black one for any changes you wish to make to the text.

This is your very last chance to improve or change your work. You are usually allowed changes of up to 10 per cent of the entire book, but after this you are charged for resetting costs. 10 per cent may seem quite a lot at first glance. However, it includes all the typesetting that will have to be redone as a result of your change. Inserting a couple of lines could mean that an entire chapter has to be reset. So if you find you have forgotten to include something important, try to make sure it means the minimum resetting by cutting something else in the same paragraph. It is usually possible to do some rewording so that you end up with more or less the same number of words.

Apart from the costs involved, major resetting of type will mean that the production of the book is delayed. Publishers plan well ahead, and a delay could throw their timetable completely. Authors who call for such major changes are not popular.

You will sometimes be given two copies of proofs, one for you to mark up and return, the other to keep. Mark up both sets so that you have a record, particularly of any changes you may make.

It's important that you return the proofs on time. If, for any reason, you are unavoidably prevented from doing so, ring your editor and explain what has happened. If you are returning the proofs by post, ask the publisher if they should be sent by recorded delivery. Usually they prefer this, and will reimburse you with the cost.

Publicity

Publicity with cookery books, particularly first ones, is very important. The publishing house may have its own publicity department or may employ an outside consultancy. When you meet the press officer, or even before, have a short piece of background information on yourself and your book ready.

This should include what the book is about (don't assume they will have read it), why you wrote it, what it offers readers and who those readers are. You also need to add some information that will lift you out of the general run of authors. Have you done anything really interesting that can be linked with your book? Fed famous people, cooked in weird places, achieved a fantastic feat? If you have a reputation in another field, a famous relation, or anything remarkable about you at all, note it down as it will almost certainly be useful.

Unless there is something very special about them or their book, first time authors are unlikely to be given a launching party. If you wanted to arrange one, however, your publishers would probably be delighted. If it is something unusual, and the food you provided from recipes in your book really delicious, you might well get some worthwhile mentions in the press.

Remember, though, that reviewers are unlikely to want to travel very far from London unless they are being offered a really outstanding experience and their journey is being made easy. If you live outside London, inviting the local press to sample some of your recipes can really pay dividends.

The press officer will prepare a list of reviewers to whom copies of your book will be sent. Your comments should be invited on it. If you know of any journalist likely to write about your book, make sure his name is included and check that all your local newspapers are on the list.

Following up press releases can help generate publicity. Your publisher's press officer may be happy for you to do this yourself with your local papers and radio station or stations. You are much more likely to get a positive response than they are. Most regional press are very helpful to first time writers. When you produce your second, third and subsequent books they get much more blasé, so don't miss this first opportunity.

Contact with local booksellers

Also, make sure you give details of local booksellers to your publisher so that their sales representative can call and draw their attention to a book from a local author. Pop in yourself and make sure they know about your book and offer to sign copies. They are unlikely to want a signing session but most booksellers will feature copies of books that have been signed by the author, particularly a local one, and anything that picks your book out from the general throng is valuable.

Once your book has been published, pop into any bookshop you pass and look for it. If you see it, take it and any other copies to the owner or manager and ask if they'd like them signed. Usually they will be delighted. The only exception I've ever come across was a Parisian bookshop where I found my *Little French Cookbook* and they appeared very surprised at the notion that anyone would want a book signed by the author. Perhaps the French don't bother. In America, where I've found that particular book all over, signed copies are as popular as they are in the U.K.

If your book isn't being stocked, find the owner or manager and ask if they know about it. Again, booksellers, particularly independents that aren't part of a chain, are almost always delighted to talk to authors and will happily chat, sometimes explaining why they can't stock your book! But you may well have made a sale. The best experience is when you hear that they have just sold out of your book, have reordered and are waiting for more copies.

If your book is recipe based, the specialist bookshop, Books for Cooks, holds occasional author sessions on Saturday mornings. The author goes along with samples of food prepared from the book, arranges these on a table along with a pile of the books the shop has ordered, then offers customers a bite to eat. It's great fun and can sell a satisfactory number of books. You may be able to arrange a session, or suggest a similar idea to another bookshop – perhaps your local one.

Demonstrations

If you have any experience in demonstrating cookery, there may be places such as kitchen shops which will be happy to invite you to give a demonstration at which you can sell your book. Usually this will be without a fee or even expenses.

Charities are always looking for ideas for fund-raising events and so a cookery demonstration is often welcome, particularly if the demonstrator waives a fee and asks if books can be sold at the end instead. Recipe sheets need to be provided; if you can type them out, the charity will usually arrange for them to be copied, and your expenses should be reimbursed.

As far as equipment is concerned, if an adequate audience can be guaranteed, the local Gas Board will sometimes agree to provide a stove and demonstration counter. I manage to be self-sufficient with a two-ring electric hob and a small, portable oven that operates off an ordinary 13 amp power point. Overhead mirrors are helpful but not essential.

121

Readers' letters and problems

When your work is published, particularly if it is recipe based, you may well have feedback from readers.

When I was writing for the *Daily Telegraph*, I used to get delightful letters saying how much the reader had enjoyed recipes, sometimes giving me one they thought I'd be interested in, and often asking for information on some aspect of cooking. Occasionally, the reader had run into trouble when preparing my recipe and wanted to know what had gone wrong.

I always like to answer reader's letters as soon and as fully as possible. Sometimes it's best to discuss a problem over the telephone, as only then can you identify exactly why they had been having trouble. I remember one reader who was convinced a biscuit recipe had to be wrong and needed much more flour to work properly. It was only when I asked about her oven that we identified a faulty thermostat as the root of the problem. After the oven was heated to the proper temperature, the biscuits came out perfectly.

Sometimes you don't have the answer to a problem at your finger tips and it is necessary to research further. That is always interesting and you find that manufacturers and experts of all sorts are very happy to give you information and discuss various aspects of food and cooking. Your knowledge expands along with that of your readers and you may get ideas for future articles as well.

Writing regularly for a magazine or newspaper generates more mail than books or the odd article. It is great fun to establish a relationship with readers but this also carries a responsibility. Readers can come to look on you as almost a family friend and you have to be careful not to get too involved.

PLR

Many authors enjoy returns from Public Lending Rights. If your book is ordered by libraries, make sure you register for

PLR. Write for a form to: PLR, Bayheath House, Prince Regent Street, Stockton-on-Tees, Cleveland TS18 1DF. Telephone: 0642 604699. The only cost is postage.

The future

Getting articles published is often a first stage to getting a book accepted. After your first book has been accepted, start thinking of an idea for your second. By the time your book is on the shelves and being bought by readers, you could have sold the synopsis and be working on the text of the next. That is the ideal. Things don't always work out that way – but as long as you keep producing ideas for both articles and books, things will eventually start slotting into place. Persistence pays every time.

11

SELF-PUBLISHING

There are a number of writers who have successfully taken the self-publishing path. Some have been frustrated at their inability to interest commercial publishers in their work. Others just want a simple volume printed, perhaps to sell in aid of a charity and not the sort of thing that would interest a publisher. Or they want the fun of producing and marketing a book that is all their own work. If it meets a real need, or fills a specialist niche, it can be quite easy to sell. Lastly, there are those who want to produce an inexpensive book to give away. It could prove a very nice sample of an otherwise unpublished cookery writer's work.

The main danger to remember is that, if you are very ambitious, printing can involve large sums of money, sometimes thousands of pounds. It may take a long time to sell enough copies to cover your outlay and it is more than possible that you may never get it back. Even if your aims are quite modest, you are still going to have to invest what will probably be at least several hundred pounds.

Self-publishing, in fact, is not something to be rushed into. Before you even start approaching printers for quotations, you would be wise to read up as much as you can on the subject. Peter Finch's book *How to Publish Yourself* (Allison and Busby), is a good place to start and your library can suggest others.

These are the main points to consider:

- Marketing possibilities
- Text

- Illustrations
- Binding and cover
- Print run and market research
- Choosing a printer
- Getting a quotation
- ISBNs and other wrinkles
- Selling price
- Selling your book
- Publicity

Marketing possibilities

The first consideration before entering self-publishing must be: will you be able to sell your book?

Small books, inexpensively produced, can be sold quite successfully *if* a market for them exists.

Have you a ready-made list of customers, such as supporters of a charity? Would your book supply the needs of a niche market? Do you know that you can sell your book through craft fairs or demonstrations? Has it a regional interest that isn't covered by anyone else that could mean local booksellers would stock it? If you can answer 'yes' to any of these questions, you may be able to self-publish and sell enough books to cover your costs, maybe even at a profit.

If, however, you are more ambitious and are looking to see your book in general booksellers, alongside volumes produced by commercial publishers, the questions become much harder. Your book has to look good enough to compete successfully for the attention of both the bookseller and the reader. The production costs will almost certainly be higher and the problem of selling your book much greater.

If you have been approaching publishing houses without success, look at why they have been turning down your manuscript. It has been said that any book that has a real market will eventually be taken on. *Does* yours have one? Is there a valid reason why it hasn't been accepted?

Margaret Shaida, author of *The Legendary Cuisine of Persia* (Lieuse Publications), found that publishers liked her script very much. But they wouldn't take it on, even though it was the first to cover Persian food comprehensively in English, because they felt there weren't enough people interested in Iranian food to justify publishing such an expensive book.

Margaret felt the market was there. Many Iranians had fled their country at the time of the Shah's downfall. Their children, brought up on Persian food, were leaving home needing a cookery book. There were English women married, like her, to an Iranian, who wanted to be able to cook traditional food for their husband and children. And there were many people interested in the culture and cuisine of different countries who would welcome a well-researched account of Persian food.

Margaret knew she had a book worth publishing and she was convinced it had a market. So she and her husband decided to publish it themselves. They were helped by the fact that their experience with magazines meant they knew how to set about producing the book and could personally undertake some of the work. They decided to go for a top quality hardback, beautifully designed and produced with eight colour photographs. Their confidence has been justified. The book won the 1993 Glenfiddich Award for Best Cookery Book of the Year and the paperback rights have now been sold to Penguin. Even with this success, however, it will take time for them to recoup their costs.

Assess your market together with your book. Can you produce an attractive volume at a price people will be prepared to pay and are there enough people who will buy copies to cover your costs and make the profit you look for?

Text

A manuscript undergoes various stages before it becomes a book. Design work is carried out to decide the typeface to be used, the look of the page, how any illustrations will be included and other matters. Then the text is typeset, illustrations slotted in and camera-ready artwork prepared. After this, the book is ready to be printed. Each of these stages involves different costs and some of the stages needn't be performed by a printer.

Look first at your text. The longer a book is, the more expensive it is to produce. Can you cut your work? Are you repeating yourself and including irrelevant information, or taking too long to make a point? Work is often improved by ruthless editing. Think also about the type font to be used and the amount of space you would like your text to occupy on the page and the size of that page. Though your book should look good to attract the reader, it needn't use space extravagantly.

Make sure the text of your book, when printed, will run to multiples of either sixteen or thirty-two, according to page size and the printer's machinery. Odd pages can bump up costs and it is usually easy to manipulate text to make it fit.

A handwritten text takes much longer to typeset than a typed one and therefore costs more. If you aren't a typist yourself, it will probably pay you to have it typed by a professional before delivery to the printer.

You may, though, have wonderful handwriting and be interested in producing a book in which the text appears as you have written it. There have been a number of successful books produced this way by commercial publishers. It can look very attractive (*see* Chapter Nine), but will probably cost more to have printed.

If a book were just a collection of printed words, we could all parcel up our typescripts and sell them. But a book has to be designed. It should give pleasure to look at as well to read. And if it's a cookery book, it must be easy to use as well.

Cookery books are more difficult to design than, say, a novel, where the words flow without any interruption other than that of chapter headings. Lists of ingredients need presentation and care has to be taken to see readers don't have to turn a page to follow a recipe.

More care has to be taken over highlighting such things as recipe watchpoints, accompaniments, or freezer and micro- wave instructions.

You may need symbols for illustrating the time and cost involved for each recipe, or perhaps the level of skill in- volved, or whether the dish will freeze and other information. Perhaps a glossary is necessary – and you will certainly need an index.

Before you see a printer, you need to have a very clear idea of what you want your book to look like and a manuscript that is presented in as finished a form as possible.

Illustrations

Does your book need illustrations? They will add to the cost. If they are essential, think about what *sort* of illustrations (look again at Chapter Nine). The production costs for black and white drawings will be cheaper than for photographs, and any sort of monochrome illustration will be much cheaper than full colour.

The manuscript should show exactly where the illustration should be placed. Use some sort of identification code that can be repeated on the back of the right illustration. Make sure captions are included.

Binding and cover

Your cover is what will initially sell your book. It needs to be as attractive as possible and give a flavour of the book's contents. Sort out what you want before visiting a printer. Have a mock-up made which includes the book's title and all the other information you want on it. Make sure the sketch uses the size of lettering you want.

A simple, coloured card cover, printed in a toning or contrasting single colour, can look very attractive and will cost a fraction of a colour print.

A stiff paperback type of cover can be printed in full colour and can even sport a dustjacket with inside flaps for giving the reader information about the book; what is usually known as the 'blurb'. Or the back cover can carry all the necessary information.

A hardback cover will cost a great deal more than a card cover and will look best with a colourful dust jacket. It adds to a book's prestige and shelf life but also to its cost.

If your book is quite short, perhaps produced to sell locally, a staple binding will cost very much less than a proper book binding and could prove acceptable.

Spiral binding is an option particularly suited to inexpensive cookery works as it helps the book lie open at the right page.

Avoid a cheap glue binding. The pages will soon start coming adrift – very unsatisfactory for a recipe book that will be constantly in use.

The better your binding, the more easily your book will open, the longer it will last, the better it looks and the more expensive it will be. You can ask your printer to quote for various types of binding.

Print run and market research

One of the most difficult areas in assessing costs is to decide the print run of a book. The more copies you have printed at the same time, the cheaper the cost of each individual book but the more room you need to store the books and the larger the market you need to have in order to sell them. And, of course, the more money you have to pay the printer.

Some printers offer a warehouse facility for storing books until they are needed. The cost is usually quite high but, if you are dealing in large numbers, it could be worthwhile, as books can take up a considerable amount of space. Also, storage has to be at the right temperature and humidity if the books aren't to deteriorate.

Having only a percentage of your print run bound can be a useful option. Binding usually represents a sizeable percentage of a book's costs and it can be quite easy to get binding done in comparatively small numbers, say a few hundred. You could have, for instance, 2,000 copies printed but only 25 per cent bound to begin with. The pages will have to be stored by the printer to ensure they will be usable later on but the economics could be attractive.

How busy is your printer? Could your book be quick and easy to reprint? What would it cost? Would you be wise to under rather than over-estimate your market and order more copies if your book looks like being a run-away success? Remember, you are entitled to the negatives your printer has prepared from the camera-ready artwork. If your original printer is too busy to do a rerun, you may be able to find another prepared to fulfil your order quickly.

Do as much market research as you can before deciding on your print run.

Librarians can help you to find the national size of many special interest groups, such as vegetarians. Often, these statistics are expressed as a percentage of the population. If you are intending to sell primarily in your area, you can apply the same percentage as the national to your regional population and get a rough idea of the size of the local group, unless your area has some special variation. Then, check to see whether or not their needs are already being supplied.

Finding others who have successfully self-published can be of great benefit. Your local library may be able to help. Printers may be able to show you self-published books. Very often the publisher's address in the book will be that of the author. Local charities may have produced a recipe book to raise funds. Or someone you know may be able to come up with a name.

Try to be realistic when assessing the size of your market. First cookery books by unknown writers are often lucky to sell 1,500 copies in hardback even when they're published by a well-known house and given the benefit of a national sales and distribution team plus a professional publicity campaign. If you are doing all the selling yourself, you are going to have to work very hard to do as well.

If you are having a booklet printed at one of the high street design and print bureaux, there is a possibility that you can have small numbers photocopied, even as little as twenty or thirty. You still have to pay for design and camera-ready artwork but this method could cut down dramatically on printing costs. See next section for more detail.

Choosing a printer

There are three main options available for getting your book printed:

- A commercial printer
- A high street design and print bureau
- A computer with a Desk Top Publishing programme plus one of the above

Commercial printer

A commercial printer is the traditional method. He may well print books for large publishers and can produce a book to compete with others in a bookshop. He may have an in-house designer but is more likely to use a freelance. He will discuss all aspects of your book and its production with you, including design, cover and binding. His machines can vary from the most modern and up-to-date to very old-fashioned, so his prices and, probably, delivery dates will reflect his type of machinery. Some printers can use customer-supplied disks, which cut out the typesetting and proof reading stages (*see* Desk Top Publishing below).

If you are looking at a high quality book with colour pages, foreign printers are usually more competitive. Consult small publishers for details; given the right approach, they can be very helpful.

A high street design and print bureau

A high street design and print bureau will work with modern computer equipment and scanners that can typeset and drop illustrations into text on a disk ready for camera-ready artwork. At some bureaux, you can work with their designers on your text and see it take shape on the screen.

The print bureaux usually use laser printers to produce camera-ready artwork. This will then be photocopied rather than printed, which can make the production of a simple booklet of, say, twenty pages, very economical. Your initial costs are the same but small numbers can be run off on a photocopier very cheaply. With a card cover and staple binding, you can have a result that looks attractive and will sell at a very reasonable price. Selling one batch could finance the production of another. Remember, though, that photocopied pages eventually fade.

A computer with a desk top publishing programme plus one of the above

With desk top publishing you are looking at designing and typesetting your book yourself on a computer equipped with a desk top publishing programme. Your disk is then handed to a printer or bureau to produce camera-ready artwork and print your book, cutting out design and typesetting costs. Before embarking on such a process, you should check that your programme and your disk will be acceptable to a printer.

Getting a quotation

Once you have sorted out exactly what you want, ask printers to submit quotations. Always approach at least two and preferably three printers, checking details in Yellow Pages. Make sure your selection includes a modern company with up-to-date equipment and a smaller, perhaps old-fashioned type of company. You may also like to look at the possibilities of approaching a high street design and print bureau, particularly if your book is going to be quite short.

Make sure you give the companies identical specifications so that you can compare like with like.

If you know a book designer, you could ask him to quote and ask the printers for two quotations; one which includes the design element and one which doesn't.

It can be difficult to find the right printer. Do your homework beforehand, and learn as much about the procedure as possible. Then query every suggestion made, particularly if the book looks like costing more than similar books already on sale. Ask which kind of paper will be cheapest as well as most suitable. Query design and typesetting costs. Investigate covers and bindings.

If you are not VAT registered, you need to look at the effect these regulations can have on how you get invoiced for the printing of your book.

At the time of writing, books are not subject to VAT. But only the company producing the end product is able to issue you an invoice without adding VAT. Freelance designers and typesetters, etc., who are VAT registered will have to add it to any invoices they send you and you will have to be registered yourself to get it back. Likewise, under present regulation, if you ask a printer to quote, including delivery, no VAT will be added to the invoice. If, though, you ask for the job to be quoted without delivery, intending to pick up the consignment yourself, and then change your mind after the job has been done, the delivery charge will be separate and will have to have VAT added.

Printers usually quote firm for a certain length of time, say sixty days, with paper and materials subject to variation. It is best to go through the quotation again at the time of ordering (particularly if some time has elapsed between receiving the quote and delivering your copy), to check that costs remain the same.

ISBN number and other wrinkles

You have probably noticed that all books today have, both on their back cover and inside, an ISBN. This is the International Standard Book Number, specially allocated to that particular book, which is used by booksellers and librarians. ISBNs are issued, free of charge, by: Standard Book Numbering Agency, 12 Dyott Street, London WC1A 1DF. If you write, giving the details of your proposed book, you should receive your ISBN by return. Most printers, though, are prepared to arrange the number for you if you prefer.

It is also possible to get the number converted into a bar code. This is useful if you expect the book to sell through bookshops since it makes their invoicing and stocktaking easier. Again, a printer can arrange this for you.

Under the Copyright Acts the following libraries are entitled to a free copy of your book: The British Library; the Bodleian Library, Oxford; The University Library, Cambridge; The National Library of Scotland; the Library of Trinity College, Dublin; and the National Library of Wales. The copy for the British Library should be sent to the Legal Deposit Office, the British Library, Boston Spa, Wetherby, West Yorkshire LS23 7BY. For the other libraries, contact their agent: Mr A. T. Smail, 100 Euston Street, London NW1 2HQ, telephone: 071 388 5061 and ask for details of how many copies he requires.

Any procedure which can help your book get into libraries is worthwhile (even though it involves sending out a few free copies). Being included on data banks ensures your book reaches a wider market. If your book is ordered by libraries, make sure you register for PLR (*see* previous chapter).

All books have to include details of their publisher, so find a good name for yourself. It looks more professional than using your own name, especially when it comes to marketing and promotion. A favourite ploy is to use the name of one's house or village with 'Publishing' after it.

Selling price

When you are working out the selling price of your book, you have to take into account more than printing costs. You are now a publisher and will have to pay postage, packing and delivery on your books. Bookshops will expect a discount on the selling price of at least 33 per cent. If you can find a representative and distributor to take your book on, they will expect some 26 per cent, while a distributor alone will net 12½ per cent (check Cassell's *Directory of Publishing*, trade section, and classified ads in the book press for names and addresses to approach). Many booksellers will only take your book on a 'sale or return' basis and, in any case, will expect ninety days credit. Then there is interest on any bank loan or non-interest on the money you have tied up in the book, not to mention the time you have invested in producing your work, together with its promotion and the administration involved. Standard advice on pricing a book is to take the unit cost and multiply it by four. Even if you are not going to sell through booksellers, advertising and promotion will probably match their 33 per cent discount.

Selling your book

This is the part that many people find tedious and others fascinating. It is undoubtedly very hard work.

You are the best person to sell your book. Representatives and distributors, if you can get them interested, will be dealing with many other books in addition to yours. Only *you* can give it the individual attention it needs to be successful.

Booksellers need to be approached personally, by phone or in person. If the latter, have copies ready to leave with them. Independent booksellers are likely to be more responsive than multiples, though if you can interest the head buyer of a chain in taking on your book, it is worth a great deal.

If your book reaches a niche market there may well be

some publication devoted to it. It is almost certainly worth advertising in such a journal. How large an advertisement will depend on the cost and what you feel its potential is worth. An order form, as part of the advertisement, could well pay off. Only specialised advertising of this sort is likely to be cost-effective.

There may be a society, or several societies, whose members could be interested in your book. See if you can arrange for a mailing to be sent to them. Build up mailing lists from as many sources as you can organise. Investigate Post Office schemes for first time and other mailings. A simple leaflet describing your book and incorporating a tear-off order form is not expensive to produce and could be useful in many ways.

Craft fairs and markets could offer possibilities.

Offering local societies a talk on your speciality, or a cookery demonstration, could be another way of bringing your book to public notice. Many societies are very willing for books to be sold by the author after a talk, particularly if they haven't had to pay a lecture fee.

Publicity

The best sales aid you can give your book is publicity. A good mention in the press is worth much more than an advertisement and it won't cost you more than the wholesale cost of the book plus some postage.

Send review copies to all the publications you feel might be interested. Enclose with it a one-page release giving a very short description of the book, an interesting detail or two on its author plus full details of the publication date (which can be any date you like but a Thursday is usually used by the big publishing houses), price, author's name and the name you've dreamed up for the publisher plus address and telephone number.

Ring up local press and radio stations. Ask if your book

has arrived then try and interest them in an interview. Have an angle ready you think could be particularly suitable. You will probably find them very responsive, especially if you sound lively, interesting and articulate. Read the section about publicity in the last chapter.

Vanity publishing

There are companies who offer to publish books at the author's cost. Their promises are usually inflated beyond their ability or intention to perform. Very little effort is put behind selling the books and often the author finds that though the contract specifies so many copies to be printed, not all have to be bound. He therefore doesn't even have the full complement of books available to sell himself without spending a great deal more money. There are so many warnings given against this type of publishing, it is a wonder the companies survive in business. If you are going to pay to have your book published, it is better to handle the whole project yourself.

APPENDIX

Writers' handbooks. New editions published each year:
The Writer's Handbook, published by Macmillan, London
Writers' & Artists' Yearbook, published by A & C Black, London

Book shops which specialise in food and cookery, stocking both new and secondhand books:

Books for Cooks, 4 Blenheim Crescent, London W11 1NN.
    Telephone: 071 221 1992 and 071 221 8102
The Cook's Bookshop, Scobie & Mackintosh, Bankhead Avenue, Edinburgh EH11 4BA
    Telephone: 031 458 5500
    Fax: 031 458 5412

Antiquarian and secondhand booksellers specialising in Gastronomy, all of them send out regular catalogues. Telephone for an appointment if you wish to call:

Janet Clarke, 3 Woodside Cottages, Freshford, Bath BA3 6EJ
    Telephone: 0225 723186
    Fax: 0225 722063
Global Gourmets (Clarisa Dickson Wright and Henry Crichton-Stuart), 43 Argyle Place, Edingburgh EH9 1JT
    Telephone: 031 221 1101
    Fax: 031 229 4747
Simon Gough, 3 Fish Hill, Holt, Norfolk NR25 6BD
    Telephone: 0263 712650/712761
    Fax: 712276
Tom Jackson, 22 Parish Ghyll Road, Ilkley, Yorkshire LS29 9NE
    Telephone: 0943 601947
John Lyle, 3 Faubourg Saint Roch, 34620 Puisserguier, France
    Telephone: 010 33 67 93 82 44

APPENDIX

Cooks Books (T. & M. McKirdy), 34 Marine Drive, Rottingdean, Sussex BN2 7HQ
   Telephone: 0273 302707
   Fax: 0273 301651
Ann Morgan-Hughes, Meadow Cottage, High Road, Wortwell, Nr Harleston, Norfolk IP20 0EN
   Telephone: 0986 788826
Liz Seeber, 10 The Plantation, London SE3 0AB
   Telephone: 081 852 7807
   Fax: 081 318 4675

Enquiries regarding the Guild of Food Writers should be sent to:
Christine Thomas, The Administrator, Guild of Food Writers, 48 Crabtree Lane, London SW6 6LW
   Telephone and Fax: 071 610 1180

INDEX

INDEX

INDEX